Was it Something I Said?

*For my father, Tony Thomas
Once doomed to be a mythical creature
in my life, your daily emails are
now like oxygen.*

Ros Thomas

Was it Something I Said?

Misadventures in Suburbia

First published in 2014 by
UWA Publishing
Crawley, Western Australia 6009
www.uwap.uwa.edu.au

UWAP is an imprint of UWA Publishing
a division of The University of Western Australia

THE UNIVERSITY OF
WESTERN AUSTRALIA
Achieving International Excellence

This book is copyright. Apart from any fair dealing for the purpose of private study, research, criticism or review, as permitted under the *Copyright Act 1968*, no part may be reproduced by any process without written permission. Enquiries should be made to the publisher.

Copyright © Ros Thomas 2014

The moral right of the author has been asserted.

A full CIP entry is available from the National Library of Australia.

978-1-74258-556-7

Typeset by J & M Typesetting
Printed by Lightning Source
Cover photograph of Ros Thomas by Frances Andrijich.

FOREWORD

A very unusual event occurred one Saturday morning in my home in mid 2012. I found my wife Katie in tears at the kitchen table while reading a copy of *The Weekend West*.

What had we published that had upset her so much? It was the column she had become quickly addicted to in a few short weeks – the column written by Ros Thomas.

She later asked me for an email address for Ros and like hundreds and now thousands of West Australians sent her an email praising the honesty of the column and how it had touched her.

While I trust the impeccable judgment of my wife it was not just Katie who was giving me great feedback about our new columnist.

It seemed everywhere I went I was being told by people how much they were enjoying the new column. And it was a wide cross section of people from mums at my kids' school, politicians and even a member of the clergy.

For a newspaper editor this sort of unsolicited positive feedback about anything that you publish is both rare and valued. Any editor will tell you they are much more used to receiving complaints.

What is it that Ros does that elicits such a response from readers?

Foreword

Well I think it is a number of things.

Ros has an ability to hone in on everyday topics that are often occupying the minds of ordinary people.

She then brings a unique and often brutal honesty to that topic. Most of all she is willing to reveal so much of herself and her family in each column.

I think readers can identify with so many of the situations Ros reveals. They have similar relationships, heartaches, and triumphs in their own lives.

And of course she's not shy about throwing in a little bit of sex.

The West Australian has enjoyed being able to connect with our readers in this unique way through Ros's column.

I am sure avid readers of the column will enjoy this consolidated collection of her work and I hope new readers will enjoy the book as well and then go looking for her column each week.

Brett McCarthy
Editor, *The West Australian* newspaper

Contents

The End of Innocence   5

The Creep of Age   35

Mating Rituals   67

Childhood on the Hoof   107

The Pursuit of Happiness   139

Life: Interrupted   159

Menageries   179

Objects of Affection   203

Small Satisfactions   227

Bugbears   255

Near and Far   285

INTRODUCTION

This column has been a good friend to me.

Each week it lifts me clear of my domestic doldrums. It allows me to explore the oddities I see in suburbia and the absurdities I contend with at home.

After twenty years in radio and television I had vanished into the suburbs to have baby number three. On a rainy day in 2012, the phone rang: "We want you to write a weekly column about what women are thinking. About what it's like to give up a career for motherhood. About having it all. Or having none of it. We want you to lift the lid on ordinary life."

An old television boss got on the blower: "Are you sure you want to do this? Being a columnist means sitting at your desk each week and opening up a vein."

He was right, but the scars heal nicely. I'm always brooding on the next column. At the traffic lights, I'll scribble down notes on the stub of a parking ticket I'm hiding in the glove box. Walking to school, I'll stop and madly thumb an idea into my phone lest this thought-flower withers by the time I get home.

Writing memoir is a messy business. I feel a great obligation to be truthful to the essence of an experience, to be brutally honest about my thoughts. I don't want readers to toss me aside for being inauthentic.

Introduction

Every Saturday morning, a one-act play is staged in our kitchen—my column meets its toughest critic. It's not uncommon for my husband (and muse) to find himself on the receiving end of some gentle mockery. After his shower, he'll spread my page of the Weekend West magazine between coffee and Weetbix and fall silent as he begins to read. I feign indifference and carry on unpacking the dishwasher. But each minute, I'll study his face for signs of amusement, incredulity, or rising bile. At column's end, he'll pause for dramatic effect and then pronounce: "Very amusing, Blossom" or "Not one of your best, Blossom." Only once have I been in the doghouse (see page 98). Tolerating me is his greatest virtue.

I should mention too, that when my eldest son turned 12, I agreed not to write about him, all because another mum at school gave his hair a patronising ruffle. It was the dumbest deal I ever made—a tide of great copy ebbed away. (I console myself by occasionally slipping in one of his grunts, or a scoff, just to keep him en garde).

My greatest pleasure in the columns is the storytelling. I save up the wonderful lines I see written in weird places – the graffiti in the ladies' loo, a strange quote in a magazine at the dentist's. I store away the snippets of a spat over-heard at the checkout. At times I've dredged up the traumas I thought were peculiarly mine—the emptiness of not knowing my dad, for one—and was overwhelmed when readers wrote intimately of their own absent fathers.

I hope my stories are touchstones for those experiences we all have in common. And I hope I don't get it wrong too often. (I'm still being chastised by an 84-year-old gentleman for labelling him 'elderly').

Introduction

Full of bravado at the outset, I said to my editor: "I want to write the kind of stories a man would want to read."

"Good luck," came the reply.

To those husbands who tell me they fight over the breakfast table to read the column first: thank you.

To those wives who write to ask: "Are you sure you're not married to my husband?!"—I'm afraid not. One is all I can handle.

THE END OF INNOCENCE

CLOSE ENCOUNTERS

More bosses have asked me to take my top off than I care to remember.

Back in the 1980s. Actually, it was the '90s as well.

Radio then was loose and fast and a hotbed of lascivious ego. Lotharios stalked the corridors (the best ones were in advertising) and were good at brushing up against you as you passed them in doorways. Men old enough to be your granddad offered up their laps if there weren't enough chairs round the IBM to sub your story. The kitchen was a dangerous place to be after an executive lunch, and the gent's toilet door was often left ajar to give you a tantalising glimpse of what you were missing. Perhaps disinfectant.

If you had a nice bum it got pinched, if you didn't, a smile might win you one anyway. In their wanton eyes, it must have been a glorious time to be female. I got my first job answering the phones and making tea. I was so good at it they asked me to accompany my cups of tea into the studio and be the ditzy barrel girl for competitions. I was so bad at that they asked me to try on the new station T-shirts. Without a bra.

I'm not sure what let me down, my assets or my resistance, but either way, they asked someone else do the publicity titbits and let me do work experience in the newsroom. I was twenty, naive and unworldly but desperate to impress. I became a cadet. And the sexual politics of my first job in journalism lay spread-eagled before me.

It made for hysterical drinks with girlfriends after work on a Friday night.

There was the one gentleman who took me to lunch at a posh restaurant by the river to celebrate a ratings win, only to expect dessert in the bulrushes afterwards. Or the Don Juan who would pay for my drinks at office parties and then demand to settle the bill at the motel room he'd pre-booked across the road.

Best of all was the visiting American disc jockey who locked me in the music library so I could share his hot dog. There was no shortage of Yankee doodle in his establishment – apparently.

He was married. Come to think of it, they all were. The young single guys were the safe ones. They were trying, like me, to work their way up the ladder with all they had. Hopefully talent. The older married ones had career superiority, deep radio voices and wore the pants. With their fly undone.

I never once thought of dobbing on anyone. That would have been career suicide. And they knew it. Sexual harassment was sport and they were self-deluded enough to think that deep down we loved it. The one in the bulrushes? All he scored that day was an own goal. But he didn't speak to me for weeks afterwards. He even wrote me a poison-pen letter asking did my mother know what a tease I was?

It wasn't just me of course. I was the late bloomer in the office so goodness knows what the pretty girls had to cope with.

I discovered years after leaving one job that a girlfriend who later worked in the same office had a bulrushes story of her own, identical to mine. We got our own back by swapping notes on

The End of Innocence

his ridiculous modus operandi and laughing long and loud using our little fingers as props.

Sexual harassment was then a disease that pervaded certainly my industry, and I'm sure plenty of others. It worked its lecherous fingers into any office where men had power and women didn't. And it cared little for being caught, because power gave you immunity against any salacious dirt that some girl might dig up because she was riddled with vindictiveness, or needed a shrink.

We didn't need a shrink, all we needed was the sisterhood to do what it did best. Take the sting out, giggle uncontrollably, exchange stories, empathise. It was harassment pure and simple, and if you caved in they got to brag about it. I never heard of anyone in my line of work who was physically assaulted or hurt. At least those Casanovas were smart enough to beg for consent.

But that doesn't excuse it, does it? Or does it? In the 1980s I don't recall any protection, of the legal sort. It was *Mad Men* circa 1988. With big hair and stretch ski pants instead of coifs and twin-sets. But the pearl of wisdom I received at the time from a much-loved older (female) colleague was not to take offence, but negotiate the treacherous path of unwanted sexual advances with cheekiness. My smart mouth saved me every time. And saved my relationship with the men who really were very good at their job of teaching me. If only they'd concentrated on it hard enough.

As I got older and wiser, they became more manipulative. In Sydney, the long 1990s lunch was like quicksand – how deftly could you make your escape before you got dragged under by the cocktails they plied you with and the expensive red wine that was working its magic on them under the table.

The End of Innocence

But for every groping buffoon there were a dozen others who were a joy to work with. Colleagues and bosses throughout radio and television who were decent and professional and served as the best and most inspiring of mentors. Those who still knew how to have a good time. With their wives.

Whatever happened to the Yankee and his pals? I expect they had long and fruitful careers, and in retirement can look back fondly. On their fondles. I heard one is now calling sumo contests in Japan. Good luck propositioning one of them.

I now have a small daughter and two sons. The boys hopefully will have a good moral compass to guide them in the workplace. I hope my daughter never has to tell my kind of stories. Funny as they are, they're also a dirty scourge on the heyday of media in this country. And now I'm at home with three children I'm free to try on any promotional T-shirts. As long as they come with a built-in bra.

LOVE IN THE TIME OF LEGO

Six is a splendid age for puppy love. At dinner, I asked my small son why five-year-old Violet had taken his fancy over all the other girls in his class: 'Because she's the only one with a round head.' His older brother stifled a guffaw. But I knew what he meant, having a round head myself, unlike my children's father, who has an annoyingly square head.

My six-year-old was smitten. I watched him as he deliberated over whether to write her a love letter using red crayon or orange crayon. He settled on blue. Then he drew an elaborate aeroplane with two wings and two wheels and two little faces peering out from two windows in business class. 'To Violet' he wrote carefully and drew a box with a love heart.

'Is she so pretty?' I asked him as we walked to school. He had his letter in hand, ready for hiding in Violet's bag. 'She's as pretty as Pinocchio!' he declared proudly. I didn't have the heart to tell him Pinocchio had a really big nose and came with strings attached.

Violet asked to come to our house to play. My lad waited by the window to see what colour car she had: 'White!' he yelled to me, 'It's bright white!'

I made a fuss and baked his favourite brownies. They sat nervously together at the kitchen bench, legs dangling, until he showed her how to swivel on her stool to make it squeak. In return, she demonstrated how she could lick the end of her nose with her tongue. He snorted and blew a cloud of icing sugar off his plate. Encouraged by her giggles, he took off his shoes and skidded across the lounge room floor in his socks, crashing noisily into the French doors. She looked over at me, alarmed (Violet only has sisters). I gave her a wink and her little baby-face relaxed into a smile. The two of them raced upstairs to play Lego.

My own taste of puppy love was carnal by comparison. In Year 4, I sat side by side with a boy called John. Our teacher, Mrs Gray, barked at us like Cornelia Frances on *The Weakest Link*. While Mrs Gray's back was turned, eight-year-old John turned to me and whispered: 'Give us a look, then!'. Never one to put risk before risqué, I gave him an eyeful of my regulation Bonds cottontails size six under the desk. I arrived at school next morning to discover he'd moved his things and was sitting at another desk with the new girl, a mystery brunette.

Puppy love can bite back. Last week, on the walk home from school through the park, my small son burst into tears. 'Everyone says I have a girlfriend', he choked. 'The boys say I'm stupid.'

I hugged him and he wiped his runny nose down my sleeve. 'Maybe those boys prefer footy', I said, but his sobs came harder and faster.

At dinner that night I decided a family discussion was in order. I nudged my eldest son: 'Your little brother has a problem – what do you think he should do?' 'Get over it', he mumbled. Dissatisfied with his disinterest, I pressed on, elbowing his father to bring to bear his lifetime of wisdom. 'Pass the peas, champ', was all he offered.

Undeterred, I described to my child what jealousy was, and how it turned people into green-eyed monsters and how everyone says mean things when they're a green-eyed monster. 'But you have green eyes all the time, Mum', he said, looking confused. So I began explaining about eye-colour and genetics, but then everyone started talking over the top of me about whether Josh Kennedy can kick sixty goals this season.

Later that night, after the children were in bed, my life-long crush took my hand and sat me down on the sofa. 'Here comes dessert!' I thought, but all I got was a dressing down: 'Back off Blossom', he began, 'He's six, for goodness sake – big deal if he cops it for being friends with a girl? It's a non-issue.'

I felt miffed, then patronised, then guilty. Had I become one of those parents I rail against: the ones who stage-manage their offspring? Call them what you want: helicopter parents, hot-house parents, over-parenting parents. Had my solicitude made my son all the more anxious? And was I teaching him to be resilient, to stand up for himself?

Maybe all he needed that Friday afternoon was a pat on the back: 'It'll be all right kiddo – hey! Let's go to the park.' That's what his father would have said.

In the car yesterday, on the way to the dentist, I asked after Violet: 'Would you like her to come over again honey?' 'Sure, Mum', came the reply, 'you can make cupcakes with her while I go to Jake's house and play Spiderman.'

UNDER THE COVERS

I learnt more about men and sex in 1985 than I should have, thanks to a book called *The Hite Report on Male Sexuality*. It was a fat, well-thumbed paperback, containing interviews with hundreds of blokes on everything from *'What Men like Women to Wear'* to *'How A Man Likes to be Seduced'*. Its pages were coffee stained at juicy junctions, underlined and exclamation marked, and I discovered a silverfish entombed near the spine in a chapter devoted to *Men's Fantasies*. ('Stop talking' featured heavily in the advice to women.)

I used to hide out with a girlfriend in a deserted corner of the university library, sitting on the floor between the compactors. There we would pore over the book we renamed 'the boy bible' absorbing every carnal secret: 'Surely they can't want us to do *that?*' If we were startled by approaching footsteps, we would slam our bible shut and, in fits of giggles, jam it back into the shelf. That book sustained us through an entire semester of Psychology 100. I can still faintly remember the sweet woody scent of its yellowing pages.

Twenty years later, with the mysteries of marital relations (mostly) solved, I've made several attempts to rediscover a copy of *The Hite Report on Male Sexuality* on the internet or in second-hand bookshops, but it's out of print. Part of me desperately

The End of Innocence

wants to be shocked anew, feel the weight of a thousand men's desires in my hands. Like all books, that one transcends time: it is the only graspable remnant of my seventeen-year-old self, hungry to learn the ways of the world.

Such is the power of the book: the cleverness of minds printed onto leaves of pulped wood and sewn to leather bindings. Or bound and glued to a paperback spine. If asked to name what things I would be most devastated to lose, my book collection would top the list.

My life is bookended by the assorted volumes of other people's imaginations in print. It began with the Golden Books read to me as a toddler in the 1970s, every one of them saved by Mum in her longing for grandchildren. My small daughter and I now read those slim little board-books with the same wonder. For me, the illustrations are instantly recognisable even after forty years of living have got in the way.

Enid Blyton, the Famous Five and the fantasy worlds of C. S. Lewis soon followed. As a teenager, I discovered the great novels, and was carried away into the villages and slums of Thomas Hardy and Dickens, curled up in my single bed at home. At thirty-five, newly divorced, I was overwhelmed reading Yann Martel's *Life of Pi*, because I too felt alone and adrift, like the boy on the boat with the tiger. Books can exalt time and place, remind you where you were in life the week you read them. Just last month, I couldn't wait to climb into bed with the new Nigella cookbook and fantasise about the gluttonous pleasures of chestnut ice-cream at the expense of the husband who gave her to me.

Stories of the death of the book are everywhere. But not once had I heard an argument that captures what it is about books I love most, until an elderly American author called Philip Zimbardo said simply: 'It is something you hold, near to your heart.' Yes! My books too, are pressed into me.

I am drawn to bookshops – there is something soothing about browsing amongst the shelves, thumbing new books, fingering embossed covers and sharp-cut edges. It's the promise of quiet escape.

Try getting sensuous with a Kindle, or an iPad – please tell me it's not the same? Friends, avid readers also, have emptied their houses of books, fed up with the clutter and dust. They tell me I won't miss the clumsy mass of my books, that electronic readers are brilliant by design and just as satisfying. I don't believe them.

Do I fear the extinction of the book? Not yet. But I fear for bookshops. I take heart knowing the internet hasn't killed off television, that television didn't wipe out radio, radio didn't hurt newspapers. Technology is changing how we read, how we buy books and store them, but I will never part with my leafy treasures.

I will, however, buy hard-to-find books on the internet, and order others online when they're half the price. But some books need to be fancied and flirted with in person. A cookbook, in particular, must be felt, studied, assessed for compatibility with the cook. If it still inspires after that first meeting in the shop, it can be bought and taken home in a stiff paper bag to be consumed with the same greedy thrill as a new lover.

I cannot imagine the day when I do not look upon a much-desired book and want to hold it as a rare and marvellous thing. I will then carry it gently to the bath, where no Kindle dares to follow.

SEX AND THE SINGLE ELEVEN-YEAR-OLD

My eleven-year-old son knows what a rubber is. He's seen me wearing one. We'd gone to the local pool so he and his best friend could let off some steam and I could do some laps. Fighting the uncooperative elastic of a white swimming cap, I was trying to force the last of my hair inside it when son number one said 'Mum, you look like a rubber' and then he and his mate fell about laughing.

Sex education is a dangerous business.

I couldn't think of a fast rejoinder. So I laughed too. And then swam up and down the pool with my rubbered head submerged in a sea of questions – does he really know what a rubber is? Does he know what it's for? And why? And how?

I didn't envy his teacher ploughing into the sex education curriculum at the end of last term. All that sniggering and stifled giggling. A little birdy told me in one class, the teacher had the kids yelling 'Penis!' and 'Vagina!' until they lost their indignity. I might try that at home. Mine's still quite undignified.

We learnt about sex the old-fashioned way. Behind the toilet block in the school playground. Where girls tittered about how gross it would be and which one of the cool gang had already let a boy get to No. 2. (No. 1 was a kiss, 4 and 5 were unthinkable.)

The End of Innocence

By the time we were thirteen, sex education was a black mark on Friday's calendar. The teacher who took it was awkward and humourless, much like those first fumbling entanglements would be. From her drawings of the male anatomy in both its incarnations, I had a handle on the mechanics (there was an apprentice I quite liked too!) but I'd heard not one word about love itself – infatuation, desire, what led to sex in the first place, and I knew from the besotted and love-struck poets on the school reading list that I was only getting half the story.

Our mothers' *Cleo* magazines threw up more questions than they answered. *Cleo* was a leap too far but the centrefolds had us in stitches. Right around the staples.

The *Playboy* stash under a girlfriend's house filled all the gaps we could imagine. And there we'd sit, poring over the pictures (no-one reads the stories) until we got a chance at a real-life encounter, or her big brother came home.

After we left school we shared everything in infinitesimal detail. No young man's performance was ever going to escape the huddled scrutiny of a clutch of young women chattering at warp speed about the ins and outs of last night's liaison.

Perhaps that's how we learnt how to behave sexually. We taught ourselves and each other about the unreliable and shifting rules of the mating game, the dangers of lust and inappropriate flirtations, the heaving burden of unrequited love, what felt right and what didn't. Some of us found Mr Right and had the happy endings, others we know met with tragedy, crushed by heartbreak or infidelity, and many are still dating, like a never-ending story.

So whose job is it to teach my son about love and sex? Yes, his teacher's. If he's concentrating hard enough and not distracted trying to impress the girls. Maybe his father, or his step-father, probably not me, if his withering look when I circle the subject is anything is to go by.

I will tell him everything I know about men and sex from a woman's perspective. That should take about three minutes. Then I'll give him my beautifully rehearsed and effusive speech on the importance of following your heart and what falling in love feels like and bore him witless until he begs for mercy.

No, he's going to learn most of it by osmosis from his mates, as have generations of teenagers before him.

He's about to turn twelve and I know he's already being bombarded with confusing messages about his sexuality from the great mass of modern media that stalks his every move: Computer games with leather-bound women so tough you can beat them up and they'll happily come back for more. Video clips that show women laid out flat like dogs begging to be used up and sent packing, with or without a bone. Magazines full of pop stars and actresses proudly telling anyone and everyone how they bump and grind and like to change partners on a Tuesday. Music that shouts angry misogyny into your earphones. Does modern male culture think it needs to reassert its wounded superiority by resorting to the age-old business of insulting young women as hoes and hookers and easy game? God knows girl(ish) celebrities make it easy for them – have you seen Rihanna lately? She might be the highest-selling digital artist in US history, but she sure knows how to look cheap.

All the dads I know are going to great pains to teach their boys the right way to treat girls, leading by example. But they're up against it when their teenagers are turning to their iPods for guidance on these matters. And what do mum and dad know anyway? The new world is awash with music and videos and games that not only justify, but glorify the exploitation and the objectification of women.

And half the time, those mixed messages are being drip fed through headphones attached to boys who take gangsta rappers at their every word, and whose parents, hearing only silence, live unwittingly in compliance.

Is feminism to blame for spawning this cult of misguided masculinity? And how do we correct it for boys coming of age? Sex education hasn't got a hope. It's still in the dark ages. And how on earth are young girls (and their parents, no less) going to navigate this mire of mixed messaging?

Fashion doesn't help. Neither does our great obsession with celebrity. All that does is make teens feel inadequate and desperate to rise above the crowd as though being famous is a destination for who you are, not what you do.

I don't know the answer, and my generation certainly hasn't provided any adaptations for the renewed symbiosis of the sexes. Talk to any woman in her thirties or forties and you'll hear the familiar complaint that men and women are still poles apart.

And the pole is part of the problem. It's a self-centred, narcissistic, fickle, unpredictable organ and women don't understand it. That's the nub of the problem. Women are every bit as fickle and unpredictable, and most of the time none of us have the balls to speak openly and honestly about why we don't get it.

Or give it. So there we lie, adolescence a distant memory, each of us on our side of the bed with this great gulf of misunderstanding breathing heavily between us.

For my eldest son (and the smaller one growing up alongside him), I hope he experiences all the rapturous highs and crushing lows that come with the search for acceptance and contentment.

Which is often what love and sex are about. I hope he cherishes the girls who will pass through his life. Above all, I want him to treat them with respect, no matter what happens.

And I hope somewhere along the line, someone perhaps older and wiser than him, will earn his respect by telling him the whole intoxicating story of sex, with all its knobs and buttons.

In case he ever has to wear a swimming cap.

LIMERENCE AND LINDT

Who's not a sucker for limerence? That electrifying but dangerously unpredictable state of being *in love*. The term 'limerence' might be unfamiliar, for good reason, because it only arrived in the dictionary in 1979. Before that we just talked about 'infatuation', or 'having a crush'. No matter, because I've always lived for its heart palpitations (and sudden weight loss) having realised that *being in love* is the most exquisite yet fleeting phase of the human condition.

My pursuit of limerence has taken up a quite considerable chunk of my life. In my twenties, finding a mate was about being in the right place at the right time (any pub on a Friday night) and spotting someone who had that indefinable 'something' (usually a bourbon and coke and a packet of Benson & Hedges).

Go back a few more years and my girlfriends and I were 'getting the hots' and hanging around at the bus stop aged sixteen hoping the boys we liked hadn't decided to ride their bikes to school. As one of our nannas used to remind us – boys are like buses – there'll always be another one along in a minute. On weekends, we'd go to a 'show' at someone's house, and if we were lucky, we'd 'get lucky' on the front lawn. (I never did Mum, I'm just generalising.)

A decade before I was born, lovers would be necking in their Hillman Hunters and Morris 1100s all over Kings Park on a Saturday night. If a boy was sweet on a girl and 'had it real bad', he'd get down on one knee, they'd get hitched, settle down and raise a couple of nippers ('sprogs' if they were accidents).

Now, I'm discovering via my friend's teenagers, or anyone too young to remember the drive-ins, that the internet has changed dating forever. The home phone is obsolete now that you 'hook up' with people on Facebook, and break up with them via text (I was shamefully way ahead of my time on that one.)

Whatever happened to flirting in person? Or making eyes at someone? Or being (pretend) shy and coquettish? Or laughing at a boy's dumb jokes because 'he's a God', as we used to say, and all of God's jokes are hilarious. (Especially the withdrawal method. And the wonder bra.)

How many hours did I spend hogging the phone with girlfriends dissecting the subtle nuances of the twenty-second call I'd had with my teenage heart-throb, Andy, who'd rung to say: 'Hello?' followed by 'Will you go round with me?' followed by 'Great. Bye'.

At sixteen I would sit on the beach all afternoon watching him surf. He was always so far out I couldn't tell which one was him – sometimes I wondered if he'd caught a wave in behind the groyne and gone home. I wasn't even that interested in boys' groins then, I just wanted the adrenalin-fuelled charge of being smitten.

At university, a lovely Greek boy would pass me little notes in the library and take me to candlelit dinners in restaurants where surf'n'turf was new-fangled and cool. (Now it's even more hip and they call it reef'n'beef.) I used to write him gushing love letters on perfumed paper and post them with those sticky little squares we used to know as stamps.

Later on, in another time warp, I wrote poetry and swooned over my French tutor, until I discovered he wasn't really Parisian but the *enfant terrible* of Midland. No more kissing frogs, but I remained a sucker for an accent, so I took up with a Norwegian one, thinking I knew it all, at age twenty-three.

These days science tells us the smell of our armpits, the symmetry of our faces, and the distance between our waists and our hips all factor in our unconscious attraction to certain members of the opposite sex.

I'm a big believer in Schopenhauer's theory of attraction. He was the nineteenth-century philosopher who believed we unwittingly seek out our 'physical' complement, because, in evolutionary terms, the search for a mate is really about the continuation of our particular gene pool. Unconsciously, we are drawn to that individual who might balance out our shortcomings in the next generation – the one person whose long legs might cancel out our stumpy ones, or whose petite ears might be given precedence over a set of wingnuts.

Unfortunately, Schopenhauer's theory ends bleakly, because he then tells us, invariably, our most suitable *physical* complement is not usually our most suitable *life-long* complement. Long-term happiness and creating robust children are like two radical, but mutually exclusive, science projects. I wonder if that's what happened in my first marriage, because the product of it has been a mostly delightful child, while his father and I became a disaster. I blame Schopenhauer. And Norwegian accents.

The End of Innocence

Second time round, I've gone for the one bloke who makes my heart thump but who clearly has my short legs and no hope of cancelling out my histrionic gene with his calm, rational one. He is without accent, has an encyclopaedic knowledge of war history, in case I ever need it, and is quite a dab hand at writing a love letter, though come to think of it, I haven't seen one of those in a while. He can also shoot a dugite with one bullet from a shotgun – at point-blank range – and has ironed every shirt he's ever worn, since telling me in 2005 I was doing it wrongly, and you have to start with the sleeves first.

I get the feeling romance is no longer a high priority in our house because only once in the last six months has that lovely man I live with remembered his (loose) commitment to affairs of the heart. Last week he announced: 'I'm ready for date night, Blossom – but let's have it at home – I've rented *Downfall*, that great Hitler movie'.

No wonder speed dating is held in such high esteem these days. Weed out the dud candidates in two minutes and you're left with a pool of genuine romantic possibility. I just wonder if hunting in the wild is a more dependable outcome, even if it takes the best part of your mating season to find who you're looking for. Those matchmakers are in a rut – packaging and controlling the rules of attraction takes half the fun out too. I'd rather drop a line in the ocean and hope some buck-wild specimen chooses my bait, than cast out in an artificial lake full of pre-selected exhibits. I'm not after small fry, I want Moby Dick.

My lifetime Lothario knows a thing or two about hosing down my romantic tendencies, seeing he brings home a box of my favourite Lindt balls on a Friday night, and then eats all the blue and red ones. I don't much like the white ones, but I appreciate that he leaves me any at all. Then he makes me a cup of tea and we settle in on 'date night' to watch Hitler's last days in his bunker. I'm already looking forward to next date night. I think he's pencilled it in for 2015.

SINGIN' THE ONLY-CHILD BLUES

'So, how many brothers and sisters do you have?' asks the school mum I'm standing with.

We'd been chatting, this new friend and I, waiting for our six-year-olds to come barrelling out of class. I feel a thud of embarrassment at her question, but I force a smile and reply: 'I'm an only child.'

I say those four words with a shrug so they'll appear weightless, but they drop between us like stones. I see on her face that peculiar mix of curiosity and suspicion. She can't hide the look I know so well.

'Wow!' she says, 'I wouldn't have picked you for one of *those*', and our conversation skids in a direction that makes me feel exposed.

'What was it like growing up?' she asks.

'Oh fine!' I reply. 'You don't know what you're missing if you never had it.'

She looks at me expectantly, waiting for more, but I'm saved by the bell as kids come swarming through doorways.

On the walk home through the park with my son, I feel a familiar pang of alienation, uneasiness at having been outed. Even as an adult, a single childhood still feels like something to hide.

The End of Innocence

My mum wanted lots of babies, but she and my dad divorced when I was three. No matter – I had a long-suffering Siamese kitten that filled the role of baby sister. I'd squeeze her into dolls' dresses and wheel her up the street imprisoned in my toy pram.

As a kid, I'm not sure I even knew what 'lonely' felt like. I was just alone, and I was very good at it. Inventing ways to compete against myself turned into elaborate tests of endurance. (I was a fierce opponent.) My nanna gave me a plastic kitchen timer which I put to work, furiously pedalling my blue bike around the block, trying to beat yesterday's record.

Obstacle courses were my specialty. I mapped them out with an eight-year-old's precision: start at the thunderbox, swing once around the Hills Hoist, sprint to the back fence, twice down the slide and leap onto the verandah to finish. Fifty-three seconds – not quick enough. (Losers got eaten by the crocodiles that lived in the cracks in the pavement.)

We had little spare money for toys, so I grew expert at collecting odd things. I sorted buttons by colour into glass jars and curated coin exhibitions on bedspreads. I invited beetles into plastic containers fitted with five-star cotton-wool day beds and leafy gazebos.

Sleeping over at my cousins' house, the noise of their big family was overwhelming. Tormented by her big brother, my girl cousin would unleash her ear-piercing shriek:

'Mum! Christopher yanked my hair!'

'I did *not*, you dobber!' he'd bellow in protest.

I'd be scared witless but secretly thrilled as he chased us down the hallway. My role was reluctant witness for when brother whacked sister, or sister pinched brother. My aunty would storm out of the kitchen with flour on her hands and shout at us over the ruckus: 'ENOUGH! All of you – outside and sort it out!'

I was worn out from the rioting but even so, I hated being detached from the herd. In the quiet at home, I'd head for my room and dive back into *The Famous Five*. Books transported me into other teeming families where I could observe the action without feeling compelled to join in.

But my favourite story was about an only child who lived in a three-storey apartment in New York, just as Mum and I had lived in a third-floor flat in South Perth. The girl in the book had strung a makeshift sign out of the window, hoping the people walking below would look up. 'Hello!' the sign said. 'Wave to me if you see this.' When we moved into a duplex, I scolded myself for not playing that game when I'd had the chance. In my teens, it dawned on me the story's theme was isolation.

In high school, I worried that a kid with no siblings would be branded a misfit. But I wasn't. Friendships came easily and I cherished girlfriends like sisters. (I still do.) But I envied their taken-for-granted solidarity with siblings. They always had someone to watch their back or take their side.

I carried into adulthood those traits often ascribed to only children: over-achieving, over sensitive, over indulged, self-centred. I've tried to rub out those tics, tried not to conform to stereotype, lest someone point a finger and say: 'See!'

Now, when I meet another only child, we make an instant connection. Feeling safe, I'll plough straight in and ask: 'Did you feel lonely growing up?' Almost always the answer is 'No', followed by a pause: 'But now that I think about it, maybe I was.'

The End of Innocence

And then I go home to my own brood of three, cavorting and messing up the lounge room and yelling: 'Mum! Come into our cubby!'

I put my childhood aside and concentrate on theirs.

IN THE PASSION PIT

Power is still the best aphrodisiac. That's why I get all a-tingle at the sight of my husband brandishing an electric drill or a whipper snipper. The mere suggestion that he has forsaken the cricket, the newspaper and his children to do a job that lessens my domestic load is guaranteed to earn him an afternoon delight. And I don't mean a visit from my mother.

Sometimes I fantasise about my bloke leaning over the kitchen sink. I like to imagine him up to his elbows in suds teaching that saucepan with the burnt-in scrambled eggs burnt into it a lesson in brute force.

I can also get steamed up watching him iron a shirt. He likes to do his ironing after a shower with a towel wrapped around his waist. I'm always captivated by the way he moves from cuff to collar instead of the other way around, though really I'm just excited that it's not me taking the creases out. Just once, I wish the towel would drop to the floor. Instead, his belly works against gravity to keep it firmly in place. (Ironing has always been a wrinkle up the sleeve of fun.)

Foreplay in a marriage is a dance of many complicated steps. It's not like the hokey-pokey we did in our single days. Back then, shaking it about after a couple of shandies at the pub was all it took to get propositioned. Now, in a long-term partnership overrun with children's swimming lessons and endless cut lunches, the matrimonial polka comes a sad second to wakeful toddlers and twelve-year-olds who can stay up later than I can. Even when the kids are finally asleep, I find it difficult to read the signals coming from the man on the sofa. If he's engrossed in the latest Economist magazine, I never know if my fortunes are looking up, or if Greece has killed off any hope of a stimulation package: mine.

A girlfriend says her husband needs to understand that foreplay starts three hours before bedtime. For her, it involves curling up on the sofa with him while they watch Stephen Fry on QI. During the show, she likes to talk about subjects that have been troubling her during the day. Vexatious questions like whether the dripping laundry tap might fix itself. After that, my girlfriend likes some hand-holding (*her* hand being held) or foot massaging (*her* feet being massaged) while they watch re-runs of his favourite show *The Sopranos*, and she asks him repeatedly whose hit-man is whose. Maybe he gets up to make them both a cup of tea because 'togetherness' is all about connecting in ways that make her the centre of (his) attention.

If he's perfectly content watching a mob hit without her, having baggsed the comfy arm of the sofa after leaving the dishes for the maid, then she's not hitting the sack with him later on. Any hopes he has of making faces with her at 10 pm sink faster than a Mafia victim in New Jersey harbour.

I'm going to make an educated guess here and say most blokes don't need foreplay. In fact, I'll take a stab in the dark and say that leaving a man in peace in front of the telly is foreplay in itself. In our house, I have learnt the Golden Rule of obtaining amorous congress: silence. Sometimes I give myself an extra

The End of Innocence

challenge and see if I can remain mute even during the ad breaks.

The only trouble with pandering to my man's love of quiet is that some nights I have no idea where I stand. He might be a prized stud, but occasionally, I like to imagine I am queen of the Stepford wives and can expect certain reward for my verbal restraint, only to discover that while I was loading the dishwasher he has hit the hay and any pleadings for a roll in it are met with: 'Go to sleep please Blossom, I have a 7 am meeting.' (Business and pleasure are mutually exclusive in our house.)

As far as I can tell, men don't talk with other men about their sex lives. If they did, they'd have worked out that women like to use sex as a reward for good behaviour. A husband who takes the kids out and leaves me in my house alone for an afternoon is in for some conjugal happiness. On the other hand, husbands who take the rubbish out then act as though they've cleaned both toilets are likely to be going to bed alone.

Men should talk more to each other – that's what the phone is for. Commiserating with mates over the mysteries of the female libido might unravel why it blows cold even after you've put the bins on the verge. Women, of course, are enlightened about what men want because they discreetly share the details for the greater good of womankind. These are the kind of private conversations best saved for fifteen of your besties at book club.

If men had book clubs they'd have all the answers. Instead they're doomed to pub get-togethers where the talk rarely ventures outside the cricket or the nags until some bloke, half-polluted, asks wistfully: 'You know that look women get when they want sex? Me neither.'

THE CREEP
OF AGE

GETTING TO SCHOOL VIA ZIMMER FRAME

I will still be taking my youngest to primary school when I'm fifty-four.

There, I've said it.

The (laughable) truth of it.

No-one in their mid fifties should be glued by any sticky-fingered tendrils to the exhausting gusto of early childhood, but there are loads of us. Women in the full flush of motherhood interminably marching from the front door to the school gate because we started families early and finished late. Or friends who had exhilarating careers before sudden yearnings had them lining up for motherhood before the chance slipped away. And all of those who thought they'd started in time only to slide into their forties still sitting in the waiting rooms of fertility clinics trying to create those babies who just wouldn't come on their own.

My friends are amused to think that I may one day be mistaken for my daughter's grandmother.

But I don't feel any different now to how I felt when my first baby arrived two years ago.

I feel energetic, perhaps more capable, certainly more confident. Except for a gnawing sense that I am somehow less visible. Less appreciated. Because I am now just a mum at home. I'm not trying to have it all.

The Creep of Age

I worked full-time through all the early years of son number one. It was a beast of a job: it had me at its beck and call day and night, travel, deadlines, a pressure cooker. It showed no mercy if my toddler had croup and it didn't blink if I missed his kindy concert. But in return it allowed me to make a public contribution, carve out a career, use my brain and, of course, it paid the mortgage.

I look back now and wonder how I did it – taking conference calls with a whimpering two-year-old stuck to my hip, the blinding rush to get out the door on time lest I be exposed as somehow less committed than my childless colleagues – the whole time-snarled existence of it. I remember picking him up from family day care to be told he was completely toilet trained and feeling a surge of guilt and then a wave of relief that there was just one less thing to do. Sometimes I think my best parenting was done in the car, that small window of my complete and unswerving attention – singing ditties and laughing at his lisping stories.

After son number two arrived, I made a conscious decision to leave my career aside while I carved out a little niche of domestic immunity, a cocoon to grow the two littlest members of the family.

People ask me all the time: 'Are you still working?' and I tell them 'No, I'm at home' and watch them fight the frown that accompanies 'Really?'

And then they don't know what to say. And I feel forced to fill the gap with some breezy banter about the fulsomeness of life with little children while I watch them switch off. My small talk is now only entertaining to pre-schoolers.

The Creep of Age

Strangely, it's the older people I sometimes briefly befriend through the conduit of a chatty toddler that tell me how lovely it is to see a happy mother and child, and I bask in the glow of their approval. Strangers who see me for who I am, not for what I no longer do.

In the mornings, I eye the corporate mums racing through the school gate with a mixture of envy and gratefulness. Grateful I was financially able to step off the treadmill. Envious of their importance. That they'll spend their day having uninterrupted conversations with grown-ups. That they'll get to go to the loo on their own – no wriggling pre-schooler glued to their lap.

When did we tell women who are 'only mothers' that their contributions are somehow less worthwhile? That if they're not visible, they're not valuable. Because who could possibly want to mind the nest? The whole grubby-faced mess of it. On the days when I want to be productive and in control, I want to fly free of the nest too. It's demoralising. No wonder it's a rare man who puts his hand up.

Clearly I have relevance deprivation syndrome. No-one sees the work I do. The robotic monotony of home life. The house looks the same at the beginning of the day as it does at the end. Only I know how many times I have done the dishes, vacuumed up play dough. How long it takes to go to the shops with a tantrum-throwing daughter in a trolley. Why I still haven't showered by 5 pm.

Will my children appreciate the gift of an available mother? My mum had no choices. With the stigma of divorce hanging over her head, she worked like a dog to give me a good start. And now I love her all the more for it. Because it gave me the gift of a present-and-available nanna, who baked me afternoon teas, counted letterboxes on the slow walk home from school, looked for beetles in the overgrown buffalo grass. She was time rich. Will my children look back and feel nostalgic like I do? Will they remember the excitement of thundering down the hallway to the smell of biscuits?

Later on in my teens, I knew only too well the sweet loneliness of coming home to an empty house; of my single mum bound to her job never thinking she 'had it all'. How lucky I am to have a choice.

Often reminded of how brief this little window of womanly life is, I have decided to throw off my cloak of invisibility and get on with it. I have the gift of freedom, and perhaps there are as many mums out there who secretly envy me as I envy them. So I will remind myself to be glad I'm the one who gets to lift my smallest out of her cot, all baby-breath warm. I'll be grateful it's me who gets to bundle her into the pram with a biscuit and a teddy to walk the path to school we know every step of by heart. I'll try to enjoy it for what it is. Fleeting.

THE NAKED TRUTH

My days as a nudist are numbered. Last week, in the mad rush to get my brood to school on time, I streaked past my husband on the way to the laundry to collect some knickers from the drier. Normally I'd have covered up with a towel, but I was feeling frisky, so I thought I'd give him an eyeful and set him up for his day at the office.

He was sitting on a kitchen stool eating Weet-Bix, absorbed in the newspaper. He glanced up as I sashayed past. I remembered the deportment coach from school telling us that a woman's derriere is mesmerising to a man. I now get what she was on about — all that roundness and pertness, the curve of the waist giving way to the swell of the hips. So I floated by the kitchen bench on tiptoes knowing this would make my width taller and my cheeks cheekier. With a toss of my head, I shot him a wink over my shoulder.

He frowned at me and grunted: 'Charming!' (This from a man with a milk moustache on his top lip.)

Deflated, I dressed as a hessian sack and slouched with the kids to school. Pushing my pram-borne three-year-old home through the park, I deliberated: Is forty-five too old to be getting around in the? Surely a naked wife at breakfast is more titillating than the finance pages? And if I'm now too dilapidated for household displays of nakedness, then maybe I'm too old for public displays of leopard print? Or leather? Was it time for my mid-life crisis?

In pursuit of enlightenment, I detoured to the shops. While small daughter dived into an ice-cream, I propped on a bench and sat back to appreciate middle-aged women dressing their age.

Women land in frock shops like homing pigeons. They coo to each other over the new season's black and white, strutting with happiness to be in familiar territory. But the first squall of winter had willowy shop girls dressing their windows with Native American flavours – Cherokee-print cardigans, woolly and oversized and flattering only to long-legged teenagers called Pocahontas. If chunky cable knits are 'in' (borrowed by the fashionable set from their boyfriends' wardrobes), what will I look like in husband's stick-brown number with elbow patches and a shawl collar? Five kilos heavier is my guess.

But there they were queuing up for the change-rooms, champion birds in their late forties, flushed from the gym and trying on those dangly cardigans with jeans so tight I winced.

Then gliding towards me came a sixty-something fashionista. She was vacuum-packed into a black leather skirt with studs down the seams and a plunging silk blouse that exposed a valley of leathery cleavage. Two teenagers did a double take and smirked. As she passed by, I noticed that she had the golden tan of the well-rested, and gnarled toes from several decades of pointy shoes.

It takes supreme confidence to pull off a look that has other women mouthing 'Mutton!' behind your back. But she walked

The Creep of Age

with the aristocratic air of a dame who has (married) money. I admired her for the audacity of her fashion hope.

I've no such daring. I won't risk short skirts for fear of drawing attention to my callused knees. That also rules out hot-pants and dresses slit to the thigh like Sonia McMahon's. But skinny trousers make my legs look like strangled sausages, so they're out too. What's left? Aprons, overalls and peasant skirts. 'Peasant' is one thing, but I don't want to be mistaken for some wench harvesting a field of potatoes.

Up top, I have more problems. Middle-age spread is migrating from my dinner plate to my upper arms. My chest requires a pair of hammocks rigged with hawsers and struts, and the remains of my washboard stomach need to be disciplined with industrial underwear.

Then there's middle-aged cleavage: too much is cheap, but I'm not ready for a wardrobe full of turtlenecks. And don't get me started on my neck, I'm praying middle-age doesn't adorn me with a pouch like a pelican.

I no longer understand the fashion pages in *Vogue*, but the *Women's Weekly* insists on dividing women into fruit shapes – we're either top-heavy apples or bottom-heavy pears. I am an apple, but I'm only one Devonshire tea away from a pear.

Why aren't men subjected to this fashion drivel? Men are either short, or tall. Fit, fat or thin. Or average. Average is a compliment. An average woman isn't trying hard enough.

So we left the mall, my oval-shaped daughter and I, and mooched home. And that evening, I looked up the latest winter trends and discovered I should be wearing a metallic bomber jacket, a snakeskin print scarf and Frankie pants, which look like the world's tightest trackie-daks. On a forty-five-year-old mother-of-three, that's the kind of ensemble that gets muffled snorts at Coles. Until I find out who Frankie is, and whether she's an apple or a pear, I'm sticking with my peasant skirt.

SIXTY AND TOO OLD TO REGISTER

Three years ago, my local supermarket made a very smart decision. It hired an Italian blonde bombshell called Nella as a check-out chick. I use the term 'chick' loosely, because this bella donna was fifty-seven and came with an accent like Sophia Loren: 'Everything you see darlink, I owe to spaghetti.' She fast became a charismatic addition to the twelve-items-or-less aisle, so much so that a great many of the sixty-something bachelors in my suburb started favouring her express lane.

I got to know Nella because she was the friendliest face I'd seen in the service industry in quite some time. She quickly learnt my children's names: 'Buon giorno piccolini!' and they squealed 'Ciao Nella!' when they spotted her behind her cash register. In no time, she knew lots of her customers' names, and she and I had running gags about noticing each other's hairstyles when no-one else did. ('Darlink, 'e's not looking at your hair, you know.') For me, she was just the happy fix I needed after collecting yet another trolleyful of nappies and cornflakes; all with a headstrong toddler hell-bent on her own shopping expedition.

I tell you this because two months ago, Nella was told to go. No reasons given. Coincidentally, a bank of do-it-yourself checkouts arrived soon after, confounding us all with their

The Creep of Age

bleeps-ings and ding-ings. My children still scan the cash registers for Nella, but there's just the usual teenagers learning the hard way why you pack eggs on top. Buying milk and bread is no fun anymore – I miss Nella's motherly banter.

I've bumped into her near school and at the train station. Each time she recounts for me her latest rejection: 'You're not quite what we're after.' Or 'Sorry, you don't fit the job description'. She can't understand why her years of experience in the service industry count for nothing. I notice she has shed a bit of her sparkle – she's agitated about money, glum about her dwindling job prospects. I can see her self-confidence waning.

I am astounded that someone who is 'goodwill personified' cannot find a job in retail – it's because Nella is now sixty – hardly old, but positively ancient when out job-hunting. Goodness knows, she could teach those snippy young shop-girls a thing or two about being warm, efficient and polite. She'd cost the same to hire as any twenty-one-year-old, be markedly more reliable and give to her customers that lovely reach of human kindness. When shop owners call for someone 'dynamic' and 'creative', Nella is their perfect candidate, except those descriptions are now code for 'young.'

Nella inhabits society's never-land – too old to be considered an asset, too young to be cast out as unproductive and dispensable. Is it because she is seen as a greater health-and-safety risk? Or that someone her age is automatically regarded as less efficient, or unwilling to learn today's technologies? I'd imagine there are plenty of twenty-somethings showing the same tendencies (especially on Mondays).

When I was a kid, we knew all our shopkeepers' names. As it happened, our butcher's name was 'Alan Butcher' (the perfect marriage of occupation and identity). He wore a blue-and-white striped apron, had one knuckle missing and always had blood on his hands. I used to scare myself imagining him de-boning his finger but was placated by the slice of polony he always handed me over the counter. Our family and his were bonded by chops and rissoles for a decade, part of an affectionate familiarity between customer and proprietor, the kind that breeds long loyalties.

If competition between businesses is fiercer than ever, you'd think longevity in a job – the wealth of accumulated experience – would be prized. But the great swathe of baby boomers now hitting their fifties and sixties are discovering workplace ageism is now turning its prejudice towards them. Funding retirement is a scary prospect if there's little job security in middle age. How have we allowed people at the peak of their working lives to be stripped of their responsibilities, their status and, once cast out as dead wood, their dignity?

I hear stories from my mum and her girlfriends, now well into their seventies, about how they are made to feel invisible: how shop assistants and service providers look through them, past them, as though younger customers are more important. Last week, a lovely neighbour of mine in her late sixties recounted how in the queue at her favourite deli, she feels pressured to let the younger set go ahead of her, because, of course, she has nothing better to do. Out shopping, or at the bank or the post office, my mum says she now makes a point of being polite, but assertive. What really annoys her is when seniors (in her book, anyone fifteen years older than her) have their requests ignored until there's no-one else left to serve. Society needs to re-learn how to appreciate its oldies.

The Creep of Age

I've already had my first taste of ageism. Ten years ago, at the decrepit age of thirty-five, I tried to get income protection insurance to safeguard my reporting position on one of Kerry Packer's national current affairs programs. Even then, during the golden days of Kerry's empire, I was told that no-one would insure a woman of thirty-five working in television. Indeed, I'd be lucky if I was still in front of the camera much past forty. I was horrified. TV presenting is no country for old women.

I don't like what I see as a culture against ageing in this country, where younger workers are prized for their risk-taking and submissiveness and grey-haired ones are being encouraged to surrender their independence well before sixty-five.

At my favourite bra and knickers shop, one of the sales assistants would have to be seventy-five not out. I seek her out and spend a fortune there because she is the doyenne of bra fitters: the old-school kind who demands I lean over to ensure my cup does not runneth over. She is also the bosom lady who flicks her tape measure from around her neck and whips it around my chest so she can tut-tut: 'Yes, you're up another cup size, but it's because your back is getting wider.' Good grief. I can take it on the chin from her, but I don't want that kind of bad news delivered by some perky A-cup bra-girl reminding me why three children are bad for your assets. I want a matron. And she is brilliant at her job.

No-one wants to be forced into early retirement. I'd rather keel over from exhaustion than boredom. My friend Nella is not ready nor willing to be a pensioner – she wants to stay employed, play that cash register like a piano and feel good about being needed. Turning sixty should be no impediment. And if you happen to be in the market for a part-time shop-hand, Nella might just be your gal.

SLAVE TO THE BEAUTY GRIND

I am maintaining a veneer of calm, but the bathroom mirror is starting to show my age. And I'm beginning to wonder if I have a thick enough skin to grow old gracefully.

Apparently, on the cusp of forty-five, I am approaching middle age. Some would say I'm in the middle of middle age but I say their arithmetic is pessimistic. After all, I'm a glass half-full kind of person. (Usually it doesn't even take that much.)

I keep hearing forty is the new thirty, and sixty is the new fifty, and I'm confused because I just want to feel new full stop. New, as in no longer tired, new, as in carefree with shiny hair and bouncy step.

Gravity is cruel to women. We have nice bits that stick out, partly to get noticed, partly to counter-balance high heels. Sometime around forty-five, you give up stilettos because they hurt and they're impractical, so gravity decides your stick-outs are impractical too and they give up the pretence of weightlessness and down they go.

Do men feel this way about ageing? Heaven knows, my oil painting doesn't. Why would he? He knows I find his soft belly and lack of definition rather attractive. (Actually, I feel that way about anyone less defined than me.) Moreover, I think he's getting more distinguished with advancing years: he's greying around the temples and doesn't have to do anything about it.

He needs no more maintenance than ten minutes in the barber's chair once a month. Perhaps it's his absence of conceit that shows up the obsessiveness of mine.

For the first time, I have begun waxing my face instead of my body, and it hurts and it's scary. My beautician blinds me with that lamp that is brighter than a thousand suns. She pulls it down so low even the capillaries behind my eyelids try to shrink and look away. My beautician is a Nigella Lawson-styled Italian mamma, all heaving bosom and peachy skin, but she has the ability to tear hair out of me at the speed of sound. (I know this because there is a split second between when she finishes and when I let out a shriek of shock and pain.)

Don't expect sympathy from a beautician. She knows natural beauty is an oxymoron, and no-one wants to look like one of those. She also knows beauty is bloody hard work ('the longer you leave it the worse it gets'). I arrive all sheepish with my inane apology: 'I know I should have come sooner…' but she's already tut-tutting over my overgrown eyebrows and – dare I say it? – the fluff on my upper lip. I like to call it fluff because it sounds cute, like the down on a baby bird or the fuzz on a dandelion seed. Except it's not cute, it's mortifying. And then she gets out her spatula and spreads a pad of hot wax so big it covers half my face. I whine something about 'I'm not Santa Claus yet, am I?' but my question goes unheard, smothered by the tearing sound that means the wax and I have separated. My palms are clammy, which reminds me why I've only ever had one Brazilian in my whole life. (I didn't get enough horizontal Samba to make it worth a second.)

I've also started having facials. I rarely feel like a client in those places, usually I feel more like a patient – those young

The Creep of Age

lab assistants in their white tunics invariably ask: 'Will you be having the oxygen facial today?' and I want to reply 'Why? Do I look like I need to be resuscitated?' I say yes anyway, because really I've come for a power nap in a dark room with nice smells, which is rudely interrupted by a sudden blast of freezing air. It's squirted at my face from point-blank range from an air hose connected to an oxygen tank, also connected to the smooth hands of the wrinkle-free facialist. I can never tell the difference afterwards, except for the greasy wreckage of my hair and the shame of having to venture out in public with a shiny naked face.

I guess that's why it's called maintenance – the effort of preserving what you've got so you're not white-anted by sag and staleness – pounding away at the weights to stop the formerly good bits of us heading south for the winter and retiring there. Where did the rosy cheeks of my thirties go? I get them at the gym, but then it's called florid. Grey hair needs an arsenal all of its own, but repeatedly spreads like a plume of pollution, always leading from your forehead for maximum exposure.

I just don't get this ageing business, but I think it has something to do with fertility: when we are young, beauty is handed out for free so we can attract a mate and produce children who never let us sleep. After you've produced the world's cutest offspring and you're no longer good breeding stock by virtue of age and weariness, then beauty wanes, and vanity takes over. The saggy neck cream companies start trying to flog us really expensive potions we all secretly know do nothing. They can smell our desperation.

The only good thing about maintenance is that everyone has to do it. It just depends how much of a slave you want to become to it. A bit like my husband and our lawn. He knows there is nothing quite like a freshly mowed, weed-free lawn with clipped edges. I'd quite like him to think that way about me. You can tell just by looking at someone if they need a good clip, or a grease-and-oil change. How many men do you see obsessively washing and polishing their car on the front verge of a weekend? Or bending over the engine with the bonnet up and their shorts at half-mast. They know the only way to keep turning heads is with maintenance.

For some reason the need for maintenance seems more acute with women. Is it because we are the early bloomers? That we stayed peachy for so long that suddenly, somewhere past thirty-nine, it's an awful shock to discover that while our fruit is still firm, the current crop is tending towards overblown, and may, in fact, be ready to drop?

Men don't have to put up with this middle-aged demarcation because models like Anna Nicole Smith agreed to marry men who were eighty-nine, proving men get better with age. How come they get all the plaudits? We get good with age too.

I wonder why I care so much how society perceives older women – those who are keeping the fabric of multiple lives sewn together, mending fraying seams and making the stains of modern life disappear with hard work, brains and charm – why is this glorious slice of society so ignored? Fashion doesn't want to waste its painfully short attention span on dressing middle-aged women and they remain under-represented in art, photography, on stage, in cinema, on rich lists and in boardrooms. And what about bedrooms? – who knows more about how to have good sex than a woman who's been enjoying it for twenty-five years?

So, if my exterior upkeep is insurance against ever being described as dowdy, then let's do the sums here: Suppose I now spend ten-fold the time and money I spent on maintenance when I was twenty, then by the time I'm seventy, it'll be *all* I do. (At least it'll give me something to do.) And when I fall off the perch at the hairdresser's one day, my children and grandchildren will be able to take comfort in the fact I spent every last cent of their inheritance staying a natural blonde until I was ninety. And my epitaph will read: 'She didn't look a day over eighty'.

THE DECLINING DIGNITY OF AGE

I find the elderly strangely beautiful with their crepe-paper skin and dimming eyes, lined up in the sun at the nursing home.

Some of them with a busy mind but useless body. Many more with robust bodies but minds clouding inwards, leaving reason and memory beyond reach.

This is the most awful thing about the ageing process. People you know and love who have pressed forward in their lives with their cleverness, their kindness, their bravery, suddenly forced into decline. A decline that proceeds, sometimes with imperceptible slowness, sometimes at great speed, to an irreversible end.

My much-loved grandmother marched into her seventies and faded into her eighties. Small strokes robbed her of her steadiness but her refusal to be dependent kept her at home, with my mum keeping vigilant watch.

It was stressful and life-altering. My mother worked full time, I was a teenager, and at eighty-two, her mother was becoming a child.

Other family were interstate, and the responsibility was my mother's alone. She never described it as a burden, but even my immature self knew it was.

Five years went by cooking one extra dinner, popping in daily and having small panics when she took too long to answer the phone – the endless management of a life that could not manage its own.

When the time came, my nanna fought her move to the nursing home with everything she had, and my mother's guilt was palpable.

Almost every one of us has had a glimpse into the shadows of human frailty. It's not a place you ever want to go, but we'll all end up there if we can hang on long enough.

Now you hear of dementia and Alzheimer's everywhere, like it's a communicable disease. A colleague and I eat four brazil nuts a day in the hope of warding off senility (apparently, selenium is good for brain function). But with a family history of Dementia for both of us, we discuss with wry humour our dread of being the one who picks the short straw.

A lovely friend told me that caring for an elderly relative, especially a parent, forces you to change places with them. Her mum had become nurturer to her grandmother, and it was unsettling for her to no longer have a mother.

When the move to a nursing home became inevitable, she told how her mum's greatest relief was to be able to return her to her rightful place as daughter, because someone else was now doing the 'caring'.

I have just experienced again the ageing process in all its indignity with my favourite uncle, my mum's only and gifted brother.

To watch him regress to being almost infantile at the age of seventy-six was frightening, but at times quite lovely. It gave him an instant bond with my children, especially the small ones, who delighted in his gentleness and quiet concentration at their baby games.

As his dementia progressed, he became their absolute favourite for playing hide-and-seek, seeing as he hid in the same spot every time.

He was only as good at puzzles as they were, and like them, he startled at loud noises and needed help cutting up his dinner.

But the great tragedy of his twilight years was the swift unravelling of his brilliance. As a concert pianist, academic and mathematician, that disease robbed him of all he had been.

First it stole his ability to pick left from right, add up a bill or recognise a coin in his wallet. Then it took his encyclopaedic memory of music until he could no longer play a note or sing a tune.

The end came as quickly for him as it came cruelly for us, two years after diagnosis and a day after he took a rare walk around the fountain at his nursing home.

And I hear each week of another friend whose father has been diagnosed with Alzheimer's, or a mum whose intellectual decay is awaiting a name.

What is the price of longevity? And how will we pay for it?

The latest census tells us there are more than three million people aged sixty-five years and over in Australia, and the statistics tell us almost ten per cent of them have some form of dementia. That is projected to rise to thirty per cent by 2050.

You can't survive it and it's not a normal part of ageing but this slow massacre of our elderly will continue unabated until some branch of the sciences finds a way to stop it. And more importantly, reverse it.

We also have to think long and hard about dignity. Dementia can take years and years to tighten its vice-like grip on the mind.

Those who are new to the symptoms of its rude interruption to life will see their family members and friends slip quietly into the personalities of someone else. People we don't know and don't recognise.

It's as disconcerting as it is distressing. I don't ever want my mum to become somebody else. She is the bedrock from where I began, and I don't want that ground to shift because some merciless disease has changed on a whim the essence of who she is.

What are we to do? And how are we to manage? A generation of us is faced with the freedom of our empty nests being thwarted by the need to care for ageing relatives.

Do I worry about it? Of course I cannot bear the thought of my mother's decline. As a once-single mum and her only child, we have an inseparable bond.

She says she wants me to knock her on the head if she starts losing her marbles.

But it will be my great duty to care for her as she cared for me. Even though there will be days when I will hate it. And maybe hate her for it.

But I will try to push through the gloom of losing her one day by holding tight to the memories I have stored away for retrieval when the time comes.

I don't even know what's there. But I know there is a vault of them buried somewhere in the intricate folds of my mind.

As long as I can keep it.

MIRROR, MIRROR, I'M THE WRINKLIEST OF ALL

I am unrecognisable at the hairdressers. That cape of black plastic is oppressive, always one press-stud too tight at the neck. My shroud and I are pinned to my chair by a dazzling beam of expensive salon lighting. It shines down from the fashionably blacked-out ceiling and gives my skin a sickly pallor. I try to escape the kaleidoscope of mirrors by burying myself in *New Weekly*'s latest on George Clooney's beard but eventually I am forced to confront my reflection.

It's a shock to see myself: I am not this woman, am I? Is this what forty-five is supposed to look like? I notice a droop around my jawline – never spotted that before. There's a new crease in my neck, the start of some strange puckering under the chin, a deepening furrow between my eyebrows. The face I'm staring at in the mirror is a good decade older than the one I was hoping to see. Do people over forty feel as old as they look?

Which raises another question: How old *do* I feel? I've been bluffing maturity for years. Perhaps I now look weathered enough to pull it off. I like masquerading my immature self as a grown up. Doesn't every generation think it has mastered the deception of youthfulness?

So what age am I on the inside? The death of one of my best girlfriends has shattered my belief that I am guaranteed to grow old. Days after her funeral, on the most depressing of rainy afternoons, I perched on an upturned milk crate in our garage, sifting through boxes of photos I hadn't looked at in a decade. I couldn't pick out half the faces without my glasses, which was disconcerting. I got pins and needles in my foot from squatting at an uncomfortable angle. I used to sit like this by choice. But on this day, it was painfully obvious I was looking back on my past self – the girl who thought she'd always feel invincible.

There was something about those early snaps, pictures of my girlfriends and me in our early twenties at all those parties and trips away. It took me a while to work out what it was: it was a freshness, the jubilation of starting out, life abounding with potential. It was a time before we knew the meaning of illness, or tragedy or divorce. I am no longer so wildly optimistic. I'm still optimistic, energetically so, but I feel the weight of my responsibilities. I cannot imagine feeling as carefree as I did at twenty-five.

I got off the crate, packed up and wandered back into the house. My husband was taking a shower: 'How old do you feel?' I asked.

'Forty-six, of course', comes the reply, 'how could I feel anything else?' I press him further: 'Yes honey, I know your rock-hard body is forty-six, but what about your head?'

'That's an absurd question, seeing I can only feel the age that I am. If I feel thirty-five then what am I to do with the last eleven years of memories?' He had a point, but not one I wanted.

So I asked my mum. At seventy-six she is in great nick, save for the arthritis crippling her hands and feet. She comes back to me hours later, saying the question had thrown her. She felt sixty-six, she had decided. 'My body still does whatever I tell it, apart from these stupid fingers. But I've lost so many special people. That takes a huge toll. Grieving makes me feel old.'

When I was fourteen, my mum was forty-five. Our house hosted a stream of raucous visitors, the men sitting around on folding chairs with their stubbies on their knees as Mum and the other wives handed round platters of cocktail onions and smoked oysters on toothpicks. To my teenage self, her crowd seemed enviably worldly.

And yet here I am at home on yet another Saturday night, stretched out on the sofa with the cat and the weekend papers, my old man engrossed in the Tour de France. I must look like a middle-aged dullard but I don't even care.

I no longer skip down stairs two at a time. I'm scared of tripping, knowing what havoc a twisted knee would cause to family life. I'm not so fond of looking at my body (I try to avoid the rear view at all times). But if I had to take a stab at how old I feel, I'd say I feel thirty-seven. That's about the age I'd comfortably settled into my skin. I was happy. I keep that age in my head as a favourite.

Maybe I've already used up my quota of late nights. On evenings out, when I've done my hair, put on high heels and am preparing to hold a glass of champagne in each hand, I feel thirty again. Until the next morning, after five hours sleep, when I feel eighty, plus a fortnight.

BOTOX BABES ON A B-747

You know you're on a long-haul flight when the trolley dolly wakes you at 3 am to ask if you'd like the chicken curry or the braised pork. I know I'm not allowed to call her a trolley dolly anymore. It's politically incorrect. But on this occasion, it was cosmetically correct. Actually, it was probably anatomically correct.

I think she was aiming for a look somewhere between Bambi and Barbie, but she'd inadvertently ended up closer to a Cabbage Patch doll – misshapen, puffy and tending towards scary. There was more plastic in that stewardess' face than in all the little bottles I had in my toiletry bag. Her forehead was so shiny it could have shown the way to the emergency exits. I couldn't tell from her wide-eyed expression if she was looking at me with disdain, despair or delight, but I couldn't take my eyes off her, for all the wrong reasons. (Though I hasten to add she did seem very nice.)

What is going on with women and Botox? In some suburbs you're sliding scarily towards the minority if you're of a certain age and you're not tinkering and tampering with your face like it's a home-economics project. There's a veritable sewing kit of now-common procedures – from Botox needles, to fillers, plumpers, and threading – (no, I don't know what half of them are either, except I'm reliably informed the latter is *de rigeur* for shaping your eyebrows and taking years off).

I've no doubt I'm as insecure as the next woman. It's taken me forty-four years to accept that my face is an agreeable-enough reflection of who I am. Yes, I'd like to wind back the clock to that first flush of nubile, peachy-skinned womanhood, but I was too bloody insecure and self conscious to think any man who cast me a sideways glance then, was seeing anything but the flaws that loomed large in the mirror before me each morning. The closest I've come to cosmetic surgery was a week of going to bed aged fourteen with the tip of my Roman nose taped firmly to my cheeks with Band-Aids, in the vain hope it would emerge by morning as a cute, little upturned button. All I got was a nasty rash.

That said, I refuse to look down my nose at anyone who chooses botox over Oil of Olay. But I am fascinated. And increasingly so. Because botox is as trendy now as skinny jeans and ballet flats. (Or am I passé already?) It's no longer a strange quirk of celebrity pandering, but a full-blown obsession with the middle classes. (At least those rich enough to afford it.) The young flight attendants I got chatting to on a later flight told me they already felt the pressure to start on botox, given their industry was still obsessing over its appearance. And they said a medical clinic at Melbourne airport had just started offering Botox for hosties needing top-ups. Obsessed indeed.

In a hip cafe in an affluent suburb last week, I stood in line behind a fifty-something woman. She could only just move her mouth to order the fish of the day (no wonder with that trout pout) and she barely stood out in relief against the wood panelling of the counter. (I couldn't tell who had the better tan, but I think the wood panelling had a slightly more natural stain).

I'm certain she was smart and funny and kind, but I'm sad to say she looked ridiculous and eerily disconcerting. Had she left her eyes and lips alone, she would have been an attractive older woman. Now she was being tittered at behind whispering hands and eyebrows cocked above menus.

Why do women still think the only way to be measured is by their looks? Haven't we come far enough to realise there are attributes far more attractive on offer? And is it men who are prodding along this fixation with the superficial? I could be mistaken but I don't think so. No man I know wants the object of his affection to be the object of public derision. Perhaps it's our never-ending quest to remain forever young? But I think many women do it for other women. In some thinly veiled attempt to become the envy of other women. The sisterhood has turned in on itself. We have been gazumped by our own.

Women who go overboard on botox (and its family of facial additives) start to look like they're related. Have you noticed? They all have the oddly blank faces, and the fishy lips and the strange puckering around the eyes. They look like some new breed of Stepford wife. An homogenised underbelly of the middle classes with hair extensions and terracotta tans.

I'm sure anyone reading this column who has partaken of the artificial elixir of youth will be affronted by my thoughts on this subject, or worse, be mighty peeved. She will argue that she is happy with her decision and even happier with the results. And she didn't go under the knife or submit to the needle out of any insecure vanities. She just wanted to give herself a helping hand and feel all the better for it, inside and out. And I'll be so glad to hear her say that. Because I would like to be wrong. And very possibly I am.

Why then the secrecy? Why, if everyone's doing it, will no-one admit to it? I think we're lying to ourselves, and to each other, if we think anyone buys the story that we look this refreshed because we've just had a holiday in Provence. You can't rewind the clock that much. We'd all like to look good for our age, not a decade shy of it.

I admire the women content to justify their wrinkles as character lines used to illustrate a life well lived, and yet often I hear this as an act of defence, that when put on the spot, they somehow need to explain why they haven't turned to botox to stave off the inevitable.

Would I like to try it? Yes, I would. Do I know what I'm missing? No, I don't. For one simple reason – I'm too scared. Petrified of having it go wrong. I know I would rather have the flaws time is giving me than the ones some cosmetic wizard accidentally created for me.

Does that make me a coward? Absolutely. But I'm okay with that. I don't feel morally superior being au naturel and I don't feel physically inferior. But I do worry botox is going to star as the centrepiece of some sort of moral battleground – that those who don't use it will use this to take the high ground over the those who do. Is that fair? God knows I could do with a helping hand – why bother with all those skin-firming creams and potions that promise miracles you never see, when botox delivers straight-up? The pursuit of ageless beauty is forcefully marketed these days and I think even young women are feeling under siege. But what are we saying to the next generation of women if we're not prepared to age (dis)gracefully ourselves? That they must hang onto their looks at all costs? That the minute they see the first signposts of a wrinkle they must move immediately to erase it, lest anyone notice? There are few windows into the failures of cosmetic medicine. They are well hidden, unless like me, you notice them everywhere.

In the meantime, I'll try not to obsess over my reflection in front of my small daughter. I'll try not to let on about my insecurities in front of my two boys either, in case they decide it's okay to judge women by their looks alone. And I'll pray this fixation with trying to look permanently younger is just a passing fancy we'll all grow out of. And I'll have the chicken curry please.

MATING RITUALS

I'D LOVE TO MARRY MY HUSBAND

My husband doesn't want to get married. He says he doesn't believe in it. Secretly, I worry he might be saving himself for someone else.

As 'Papa' to the two smallest members of the house (and son number one, the cherished gift from my first marriage), he is the father I dreamed of giving my children. Which matters all the more because I didn't have one myself. He's also very good at being a husband. Because that's what I like to call him, even though we are not married, and probably never will be.

But I am his wife when I call his office and speak to the secretary. Sometimes I mix it up for kicks: 'Can I tell him who's calling?' 'Yes, it's his lover.' 'Who shall I say is calling?' 'Tell him it's the Minister for War.'

I like being a wife because I think it gives the job some much-needed prestige, some matrimonial gravitas. I'm just not sure I want to be called one. But I can't be over 40 and still be his girlfriend. Not after all this time. Girlfriend sounds transient, like a bit of fluff he's still toying with. I'm not the apprentice, I'm fully trained. A wife is permanent, and I am fiscally, emotionally and socially responsible for a family, and for the smooth running of the train wreck we call our home.

I don't really like the term partner either. It sounds so ambiguous. And romantically detached. I've always thought de facto was just plain ugly. It's Latin for 'existing, but not necessarily legally ordained'. That's about as dull as it gets. I'll stick with wife thanks, even if I'm not legally ordained, because really, I am a wife in every sense of the word. Except THE word. I am mother to his children. I am loyally and totally committed to him, and only him. I live with him, I share everything I have with him. (Except this column.) I hope we grow old and senile together and I live out my wifely delusions in the twin-bedded bliss of a nursing home.

It must be all those Jane Austen fantasies I still harbour about being a member of the genteel classes. But in 1816 Miss Austen wrote in a letter that 'single women have a dreadful propensity for being poor, which is one very strong argument in favour of matrimony'. And you only have to look to the insufferable Mrs Bennet in *Pride and Prejudice* to understand why she is so desperate to marry off her five daughters. No doubt they were happy to escape her as well, but marriage was for most, the only way of breaking free from the confines of family. Whether or not it was a favourable alternative, it was almost always preferable to being an old maid. And Jane Austen should know – she was 39 and never married when she published her last novel, two years before she died.

In these most modern of times, being married remains a very obvious marker of identity for society at large. They don't call it marital status for nothing. Perhaps that's why weddings are often a showy affair. I think weddings are the greatest collections of joyous people you'll ever meet (not forgetting maternity hospitals). But I'm not sure I need another one, or would want to part with our savings to have one. If only I was immune to the lure of a pretty dress – for me, that goes way back to my girlish rhapsodies raiding the dress-up box to emerge as a shining bride

That said, a marriage gives couples a starting point, a day in amongst all the other days in the great curveball of our relationships, that belongs only to them. A marriage is about the promise of happiness, the hope for a healthy satisfying cosy togetherness. Yes, it's rose-tinted to look at it that way, but when you're living in sin, there seems to be no sense of occasion to celebrate – which day do you choose – the day you met? Your first date? Your first kiss? Moving in together?

I'll be clear now that I've never wantonly sought to be a Mrs. Not even during my first marriage. I just wanted to be me. And that's what I was. No prefix. What is it about Mrs that to me, sounds so antiquated? Maybe I still don't feel old enough to be one. Mrs is what I called my friends' mothers because I wasn't mature enough to refer to them by Christian name. I wonder if it will become as obsolete as all the other colloquial terms for wife that have gone by the wayside over the years – spouse, missus, better half and (the awful) 'old lady' – because they all signal ownership, and a derogatory sense of ownership at that. It's all about whether we're connected to a man. He is a Mr whether he's a husband or not. And the absence of a ring on his left finger doesn't give it away either. Men get to keep their mystery. We don't.

You're publicly 'off the shelf' when you're a Mrs. There's no point being coquettish about it. You are, by prefix, the solid dependable type. On the other hand, Miss is sweet, until you turn 35 and then it's condescending and you sound like an old spinster who has been passed over. Good on the French deciding that Mademoiselle (Miss) was outdated. Now you're a

Madame whatever your marital status and you can't be judged on it by society or bureaucracy. French feminists have hailed it as a symbolic win for gender equality and I agree with them. Language shapes our attitudes and cultures and as a woman, and an individual, I would like to be addressed however I wish. And I don't wish to be the cheese and kisses.

Ms. at least measures up to Mr. In doctors' waiting rooms you can fill out the clipboard as Ms, knowing you're in safely ambiguous territory no matter what's wrong with you. The only way they'll work out if your better half is responsible for your ailment is if they spy a wedding ring.

Which brings me back to why I still like the idea of being a wife. Everyone knows we're a couple committed to each other and the children. But perhaps because I'm not constitutionally a wife, my soft pink, slightly insecure underbelly wonders how the man I love can really be so opposed to marriage. Well, not opposed to marriage per se (he's a very modern man) but opposed to the idea of marrying me. Maybe it's the legacy of growing up female – all those fairytale happy endings that were read to us. That Cinderella has a lot to answer for.

My paramour has joked that if ever we're in Vegas, we can hire Elvis and Priscilla costumes and get married at the Little White Chapel. I only half believe him. Though if we ever do plan a holiday to the States, I'll make sure I pack a pretty frock, just in case. And I'll make sure I cross out Mrs on the paperwork.

BETTER THAN NOTHING

I am currently experiencing the unrest of family life. My husband is working overseas. The unrest begins at 5 am. I hear 3-year-old daughter padding down the hallway. No matter the hour, she wants to celebrate her dry nappy with a trampoline party in our bed. Eventually, she drifts back to sleep but by then, I've grudgingly accepted that my day has begun.

I plod into the kitchen and squint around for a teabag, then seize the chance to write in the stillness. Six-year-old son wakes at first light because I forgot to close his blinds: 'Can we play Snap?' I silently curse the ABC for not showing Sesame Street at 5.30 am. I then feel ashamed for wishing this child had stayed asleep so I could work. Does 'having it all' mean always feeling guilty about something?

I start being a columnist when I stop being a mother – at 8 pm when I've scraped the last plate. That's when my 6-year-old finishes his homework and I give up nagging my 13-year-old son to start. It's when small daughter nods off just as Beatrix Potter's bunnies flee Mr McGregor's garden with their pockets full of radishes.

I lug her to bed. I call into the laundry, that showcase of my domestic shortcomings. I shield my eyes from the grotesquerie of baskets overflowing with sheets to be folded and shove a load of towels into the machine. I'm desperate to flop on the couch. Instead, I fire up my laptop and coax my brain into paid employment.

Maybe 'having it all' means striving for perfection and arriving at mediocrity. Maybe it's just some platitude designed to make me feel incompetent. (It's working.) Men aren't trying to 'have it all' are they? They're being told to find their 'work-life balance', which is the same thing – the pursuit of an impossibly perfect life.

I thought I 'had it all' for a few manic years in my early thirties. I'd had my first baby and scored my dream job in television. When Kerry Packer wanted a story, I didn't dare disappoint. One Saturday afternoon, my boss shouted down the phone from Sydney: 'You've got half an hour to get to the airport! Some clown's missing in the desert!'

My husband was jogging. I couldn't get hold of Mum. No time to ring anyone else. I packed a bag for my toddler and we hared off to the airport.

A charter plane sat on the tarmac with my impatient camera crew. Two-year-old boy squealed his approval. Halfway to Wiluna, I turned to see black smoke pluming from one engine. Feigning calm, I sang ditties to my son as the pilot dipped towards a makeshift runway amid an olive sea of scrub. He flared the Piper and we thumped onto a tractor-levelled strip in a deserted paddock.

We waited three hours for the rescue plane. I entertained my toddler making gravel piles by torchlight. We ate the shortbread from the ration kit and traced the arc of a passing satellite with our fingers.

After that aborted trip, I began having panic attacks. I thought I was thriving on adrenalin but I was unraveling from exhaustion and stress. How could I excel at my job and still be an A-class mother? What if I was exposed as less competent than my childless colleagues? 'Having it all' turned out to be no fun at all.

I'd like to meet the woman who's actually having it all. (I'd like to meet her husband, her nanny, and her housekeeper.) 'Having it all' now sounds like some decadent fantasy. The mothers I know who work full-time are too tired to care.

I still yearn for the profile of a journalistic career. But anytime I now bemoan my lot, my husband cries: 'Hands up if you have a martyr complex!'

I care much less about perfection. I cut corners. I've set my body clock to Play School. At 9.30 am and 4.30 pm, I jam in an hour's work while my small ones watch Big Ted goggle-eyed from the sofa. We eat boiled eggs and soldiers for tea while I picture their father ordering Peking Duck at the Manila Hilton. What if I'm now content to 'have it all' just sometimes? Sort of? Here and there? I like to reflect on those rare occasions when I've generated a flash of mothering brilliance. That morning when I ignored my deadline, the gritty floor and my tax chaos and made gingerbread with my children.

Six-year-old was fighting his sister for the snowflake cookie cutter, but I calmly headed off two tantrums by finding the six-pointed Star of David one. 'Look!' I whispered to my daughter. 'It's two triangles made into a hexagram – that's better than a snowflake!' She chose the monkey stamp instead.

That night, I sat pecking at my keyboard until 1 am making up for the lost morning of literary excellence. The most satisfying morning I'd had in weeks. To hell with having it all. I'm aiming for half way.

SPOOKED BY A LITTLE SNIP

The man of the house won't get a vasectomy. He says he doesn't have the balls.

I know he's been traumatised because years ago in Queensland, not three days after his sister gave birth to her second baby, he took his brother-in-law to get the snip. For some reason, they decided to ride their bikes to the clinic. Only one of them managed to ride the whole way home.

Mention the idea of vasectomy and plenty of men will wave you away with a casual 'Oh, it was nothing, really'. Plenty of others, however, will clutch their crotches as their eyes dart about in fear of the prospect. My better half is one of the scared-stiffs. He maintains his body is a temple and it would be sacrilegious to interfere with perfection.

The irony here is that I spent thirteen years trying to get pregnant, and the past two years hyperventilating at the thought of accidentally falling pregnant. I am forty-four after all. I've broached the subject quite a few times, thinking he'll soften up. But it's like suggesting to a prize-winning bull that he might like to lay his big swinging grass-grazers on the block just to put some cow in the back paddock at ease.

A bullock willingly giving up his bollocks? Snort!

And therein lies the great conundrum of our modern, sexually liberated lives – what to do with our bits when we've finished using them – take pot luck, take drugs, tie them up or get the snip?

In Georgia, the Democrats (of all people) introduced a Bill to make vasectomy illegal unless it is carried out to save a man from serious injury or death. (Or the constant nagging of his wife? No amendment for that.)

The Bill read: 'It is patently unfair that men avoid the rewards of unwanted fatherhood by presuming that their judgment over such matters is more valid than the judgment of the General Assembly'.

The most remarkable thing about the Bill was that a woman introduced it. And that she wanted to impose the will of government over the will of adult men.

What was she talking about? 'It's unfair that men avoid the rewards of unwanted fatherhood?' Tell that to a teenage boy who has accidentally knocked up his girlfriend. What rewards? For either of them? While you've got to admire the kids who stand up to their responsibilities and join the hard grind of fatherhood, there are many more who vanish leaving yet another young girl dependent on family or the perpetual cycle of social welfare.

The Bill went on: 'If we legislate women's bodies, it's only fair that we legislate men's. Why are you [men] under the skirts of women? I'm sure there are better places to be'.

I was always under the impression that birth control was supposed to be about giving men and women options, not taking them away. Certainly, I don't think it's my place to tell a man what to do with his body – I just hope he likes my suggestion for family planning.

I know what you're thinking: Why doesn't she deal with it? If she's so worried about it, what's she doing about it?

I'm afraid I'm doing nothing, because after years of fertility drugs and artificial hormones, not to mention my own (unpredictable) ones, I'd prefer not to add oral contraceptives or invasive devices to the mix.

My body needs a rest after the rough ride of three children. And to be frank, it's time he stepped up to the plate. He won't be sent to an early grave by the chaos of more siblings. As one girlfriend pointed out – 'the snip' sounds almost comforting – like what you do with a loose thread. And hey! There'd be a whole lot more nookie in the middle of the month. How much more incentive does he need?

A lot, apparently. Perhaps the vas deferens between us is that he was once a caveman, genetically predetermined to spread his seed as far and wide as possible to ensure the survival of his species. And despite quite an effort at evolution, modern man is still neither programmed for sexual precaution, nor to willingly give up his twig and berries to a bloke holding a scalpel.

Perhaps we should take a holiday to Cape Cod, Massachusetts. I read a urologist there is offering free pizza to anyone who gets a vasectomy in his clinic. I can almost guarantee my bloke would go for that – a one-stop shop for a super supreme (hold the salami) and sterilisation. That doctor sounds like he'd have the bedside manner to do the snip and then trot out a joke: 'Well, we're all done now and we managed to save your testicles. They're under your pillow'.

I tell my long-standing lover all would not be lost in the surgery – he might end up the lucky one-in-200,000 men for whom the procedure fails. Just ask the former school rector we know who got an unexpected delivery nine months and three weeks after his vasectomy. Being a new-fangled vicar, he declared himself 'super sperm' while his wife gestated surprise baby number four.

Birth control has always been the most fraught of subjects. Especially when it fails. I'm not looking forward to the day I have to discuss the subject with my teenagers. It will be a tough one to negotiate – will I be encouraging promiscuity if I give them the option of birth control or will I risk being negligent by not taking charge of the possibilities?

Of course, the issue of contraception carries just as much weight in a committed adult relationship. First and foremost, who is going to be responsible for it? Which brings me back to my dilemma. The man sitting next to me watching the footy maintains that fear is a non-negotiable reason to call a halt to any talk of snippage. Maybe it's because he knows vasectomy didn't start out as a lifestyle choice. In the early 1900s in Indiana, it was meted out to punish criminals, rapists and imbeciles. By the 1920s, however, it was thought to promote mental and physical rejuvenation and Sigmund Freud had one in his sixties, just to try it out. So did the poet W. B. Yeats. 'It revived my creative power' wrote Yeats in 1937, at the respectable age of sixty-nine. Stupidly, I recounted this fact to the father of my children, who with some glee retorted, 'Great! I'll wait till I'm sixty-nine then'. (That'll be the last time he gets one of those.)

I fear there will be a lot more below-the-navel gazing in our house as I seek out new persuasions for vasectomy, and my potential recipient finds new ways to sidestep the issue. I'll let you know if he capitulates and books in for the interruption of his fecundity. I've heard that time is a good anaesthetic for traumatic memory so I'll do him a favour and get his bike out of the garage in readiness. I might even pump up the tyres for him and fix the tear in the seat. That should cushion the blow for the ride home.

MUTTON DRESSED AS MAN

My husband is so fashion-forward he thinks *he*'s the new black. Apparently, the new black is a portly but cute middle-aged father of three with Henry Kissinger glasses decked out in an electric yellow Polo shirt and cargo shorts with a hammer holder.

He's not alone – I know other charismatic men of a certain age who dress smartly at the office, but who throw caution to the wind at weekends and go out in public looking like a one-man sailing regatta – all stripes and baggy, wrinkled Bermudas – convinced they're the ship's biscuit.

Or there's the dad I know who favours an oversized mustard-coloured Rugby shirt he calls 'Golden Boy' because it protects against every combination of chocolate, coffee and clumsiness. If you're a stylish woman blessed with a fashion-plate husband of your own, you'll understand where I'm coming from. Mine is more a fashion platter, an XL hunk of man who only sets foot in a clothing shop twice a year during the David Jones sales. It must have been there last summer, in the men's department, that some pretty shop assistant managed to offload some unsaleable stock by telling him: 'No, no sir, you're one of the lucky ones – your ginger hair goes with everything.' (And canary yellow was everywhere in Kazakhstan this season.)

Mating Rituals

At weekends my Beau Brummell gets around in a kaleidoscope of loud boardies and even louder shirts. The new ones are so bright they hurt my eyes. The hot-pink polo is his pet right now, closely followed by the purple one with the chlorine stains down the front. His favourite shorts are printed with a rainbow of small elephants. Friends and family never tire of taking the mick: 'Hey mate, when does the circus leave town?' but he refuses to take the bait. I fear he has become what the rag trade calls 'the technicolor middle-aged'.

Don't get me wrong, there's not an ounce of vanity living in this man. He is no ageing peacock, he couldn't care less what he looks like (obviously) nor does he give a hoot what people think. Clothes do not maketh my man, they are simply for hiding his nakedness.

I have given up trying to change him, or his clothes. I've got enough to worry about keeping my own fashion sense in check. But I bet on Saturday nights as babysitters arrive at their destinations all over town, there are wives saying to husbands: 'You're not wearing *that* are you?' All those tiffs that start with: 'I'm not going out with you dressed like *that!*' Exasperated men trying to defend why they're wearing their own 'Golden Boy' as the perfect camouflage for beer drips and gravy spills: 'Hey, I chose this to save you some washing – I'll get three wears out of this before anyone notices it's dirty.' Uncle Tony says he's learnt to save time (and marital grief) by saying: 'Okay Marg – *you* choose what I should wear.'

I pity all those blokes being asked: 'Does this dress make me look thinner or fatter?' Every woman knows this is a minefield across which no man has traversed successfully. I can see the look on my husband's face as his brain registers a no-win situation.

He's only been waiting for me for twenty minutes while I agonise over what to wear. And yet my last act of wardrobe desperation is to ask a man who's wearing a shirt with umbrellas all over it whether *my* outfit is flattering.

Those of you who think I'm being cruel should remember that I met this man when he was sporting a pair of Dunlop Volleys. I fell in love with him anyway. Since then I have had to attend all manner of social occasions on the arm of a man who thinks dressing up is wearing a cardigan.

Last Father's Day I spotted an old man's cardie in a shop selling Fair Isle jumpers and other grandfatherly attire and knew right away he would be beside himself: shawl collar, cable knit, covered buttons, deep pockets. I can't remember if it had elbow pads but I bought it anyway. As a joke. I've had to put up with him going out in it every chance he gets, with all the buttons done up. When the weather's changeable he teams it with the elephant shorts.

On occasion, my fashion smorgasbord has been clairvoyant. He came home from a business trip to Spain some years ago sporting a pair of vibrant orange sneakers: 'Mark my words, I'm way ahead of my time.' He wore them until they were in tatters, and basked in the smirks from strangers. Now neon runners are everywhere, and he likes to remind me: 'Orange is the new Matt.'

Having just moved house, I valiantly tried to cull his wardrobe. I had hopes of ushering some of the faded, torn or hopelessly stained specimens towards the Good Samaritan bin, but was intercepted with a furious: 'Move away from the cupboard.' I made a futile attempt to argue the merits of spring-cleaning but then gave up, defeated. In the end, it would be less trouble if the offending articles came with us. (Even the homeless have fashion standards.)

I have come to the conclusion that men, as they get older, realise that how they look has less and less to do with the quality of woman they attract. Partnered and forty, they stop trying to impress women by looking slick and cool because they've landed the one they want. So Monsieur begins dressing for comfort, sometimes in ways other blokes find amusing. He knows it isn't pretty but hey – he's still gets lots of sex from a woman who inexplicably still likes him.

No man ever calls himself a metro-sexual but they're out there, being lampooned by my husband and his mates. Apparently, those young blokes who've converted to man-scaping their bodies with tattoos, shaved chests and skin-tight jeans are letting the team down. In the name of research, I asked my James Bond some apparel questions as he was spread-eagled on the sofa watching *Goldfinger*. He was in smart casual: a favourite stained shirt with a pair of footy shorts last worn during the legendary University Football Club A-colts 1985 grand final. 'Would you wear skinny trousers?' 'Only if I was man-orexic.' 'How about a man-purse?' 'Yes, if you were Pussy Galore and I was armed with a Walther PPK.'

Perhaps men's fashion should be left to those who understand it. According to Oscar E. Schoeffler, the long-time fashion editor of *Esquire*: 'Never underestimate the power of what you wear. After all, there's just a small bit of you-yourself sticking out, at the collar and cuff.' What about the not-so-small bit of my man sticking out between the shirt and the shorts? His response from the sofa: 'That's the fuel tank for a sex machine.' (The bad jokes are never-ending in our house.)

I console myself that his self-esteem is rock solid. While I dress to conceal the naked truth I see in the mirror each morning, he likes to put it about in low-slung Levis and shrunken T-shirts. He still thinks I am living with a God.

So for any husbands out there wondering what piece of apparel they should make space for in the domestic wardrobe next season, my husband says the gent's waistcoat is going to make a comeback. In grey woollen flannel à la Sean Connery in *Thunderball*. I can't wait to see if he's right. Or how it's going to look with a cardigan.

KEEP THE CHANGE, DEAR, YOU NEED IT

Money is a delicate subject in our house. So delicate my husband likes to refer to me as Paris Hilton. I take offence because Paris Hilton is a vacuous party princess and I'm a down-to-earth toilet-scrubbing kind of princess, with calluses on her knees.

The laws of marriage demand we define ourselves as either Scrooge or Squanderer. Rarely are we on the same team. Agreeing on whose label is whose is a barney in itself.

Some spouses grudgingly accept they're a Scrooge because they imagine they are sensible with money. They also know a teabag can make three consecutive cups of tea if it's wrapped in plastic and kept in the fridge.

Others leap the trench and proudly embrace the title Squanderer. The Squanderer's catch-cry is: 'Keep the change!' or 'I'll take one in every colour.' They understand they may die tomorrow and never again take delight in a David Jones sale. That's how a Squanderer justifies buying three pairs of basket-weave platform sandals in buff, nude and sand.

My husband is a tightwad but doesn't know it. Secretly he loves me for being lavish and reckless. I might be a compulsive spender but that doesn't mean I'm not good with money. I run the house, the children and my wardrobe. Our phone has only been cut off once in the past year. If I forget to pay the gas bill, I just use the electric oven.

When I bought four stools for the kitchen bench, the man of the house said 'Blossom, you *do* know we only have three children?' (Doesn't he realise I like to sit down while I'm counting out his peas for dinner?)

It's a mystery to me why my Scrooge's wallet is always bulging with fifties. I like to relieve him of a few because my purse is always empty and his wallet needs clean lines. In return, he tells people: 'She's light-fingered.' Then he lectures me about how annoying it is that I never have cash, and how a Squanderer should love visiting the automatic teller: 'You won't believe it Blossom, money comes out of those things like magic!'

A girlfriend gets around her own Scrooge by telling her husband everything she buys costs twenty bucks: 'It's twenty bucks to have my hair done'; 'I got these shoes for twenty bucks!'. She's getting divorced now, but her bloke still thinks a girl's lunch costs twenty bucks.

My husband happily pays the mortgage (he calls it a 'co-habitation tax'). He buys me Lindt chocolates for our anniversary (the 'spousal levy'). Yet he can blow big sums of cash when the mood strikes him. Six years ago he paid some serious dosh for a dinghy we've only sat in three times. He bought a kayak that has seen rapids just the once (from the roof of the car), and shelled out for a top-of-the-range electric mower that snips six square metres of grass owned by the Council.

My snarky Scrooge is also a forensic accountant who knows how to bust me when I try to cover up a spending spree. I come unstuck when I forget to shred receipts or he trips over the shopping bags I've left in the hallway. It's even more embarrassing when he catches me out on my bad arithmetic. Last week I blithely waved in the direction of the new ottoman:

'Oh that thing? It was twenty-five per cent off, virtually cost price.'

'So what was the discount?'

Me (dumbstruck): 'Um, thirty-five bucks?'

Then I take the blasted ottoman back to the shop and ask for my $200 back.

I know that money goes off if you leave it on the kitchen bench. Idle cash needs to be exchanged for something new, like another juicer. Or other shiny things.

For five years, we've had an ongoing tiff about the prized soccer table I bought at auction. You remember how much fun it is flicking balls past rows of little soccer men? Well, my husband doesn't.

But the auction house was selling off the contents of the Old Raffles Hotel and I was excited. It was like being back at school and knowing the answer to everything. I repeatedly shot my hand up in the air until even the swarthy men with the big gold watches stopped bidding:

'Do I have $400? Once? Twice? SOLD! to the young lady in the tracksuit with the crying baby.'

My husband delights in telling people: 'Yes, she went to town on a crappy piece of pub history – now a soccer table is parked in the garage and my car is parked on the road.' He claims the kids have played with it ten times in five years: 'Blossom, I'm telling you for the last time – sell it!'

I suspect an ulterior motive. Yesterday, I spotted some papers in the study that look a lot like ads for second-hand caravans. He wants me to become a trailer-park wife. That, or he's planning to be a ginger nomad. Either way, the soccer table's coming with us. The kids and I can have our eleventh game while he's loading up the dinghy, the kayak and the electric mower.

NO JUSTICE IN MISCARRIAGE

I am haunted by the babies that never were. I have three children squabbling over their dinners in front of me and six positive pregnancy sticks in the freezer. I keep them there as markers of respect for who they would have been. Blue crosses in white windows, frozen in time.

This is not a column I ever wanted to write. Or thought I needed to. But the idea was planted in my head by my editor, and since then it has been growing little fingers, prodding memories of a time when all I thought of and all I wanted to be, was pregnant.

Those pregnancy tests are some of my most precious possessions, small windows of wonder at my ability to procreate. For a woman who had such trouble falling pregnant, they are reminders of the sheer elation I felt at discovering I was really, truly with child, after so many crushing disappointments and the floods of tears that accompanied them.

I know some of you will think I'm mad. Or morbid. But those three babies that didn't make it gave me nothing to hold. Nothing but the emptiness of knowing they were no longer there. A mirage. Babies who hardly had a chance to announce their arrival before they returned to the place they came from.

And so those pregnancy tests are the only proof they were fleetingly on board.

At those times, I would see the heavily pregnant women smoking outside the hospitals and want to scream at them 'Don't you know how lucky you are?' How could they be so wantonly destructive? But that's the thing about babies – they can be sturdy little souls or the most delicate of creatures and their gift is their unpredictability. They come to people who've lost hope, lost count or lost interest. Fecundity is a double-edged sword.

I have only ever talked about miscarriage in the most superficial of terms – just the bare necessities to give enough of an answer to a question: 'Yes I had one before my first son was born'. 'Yes, I had two more in my early 40s.' I don't think we've yet given ourselves permission to dive down and grind through the gut-wrenching hurt and disappointment those miscarriages gave us. For me, I struggled to think of them in any terms but failure. Yet *another* failure. Even after the euphoria of delivering two healthy babies, six years apart, two subsequent miscarriages carried the weight of even bigger, dashed expectations.

I couldn't believe I was here again. And now racing against time. That ticking clock I was so tired of hearing. It was probably just as tired of me. I tried to think of them as success instead of failure. Success with the promise of more to come, when those babies were ready to come. But the looks on the faces of those women sitting opposite me in the fertility clinics told me all I needed to know. We were all becoming increasingly desperate.

The worst thing you can tell a woman trying in vain to have a baby, is to 'relax'. It's like a kick in the stomach every time. Good luck trying to relax after years of trying to conceive and months of frantic early morning blood tests and injections on the way to work. There's nothing relaxing about it. It's a diabolical way to get pregnant.

My last miscarriage, just into my second trimester, was the nail in the coffin. The coffin of my uterus that simply could no longer sustain life. I crashed from shock, to disbelief, acceptance into despair. And anger. Mistrust. Of my body and what it couldn't do. Looking back I'm sure I had a bout of depression, but I was neither sufficiently self-aware nor emotionally programmed to recognise it. After all, I had a small child and a toddler to care for. And I was so darned lucky to have them, how could I possibly be ungrateful? And what was this driving force telling me I HAD to have another? That I just – wasn't – *finished*.

Are men as rocked by miscarriage as women? I'm sure they are, but their steadfastness and the pressure they must feel to support their partner through the awful physicality of the experience means they often keep their emotions in check. Certainly that's what happened with us. He was the rock. I crumbled.

How often do I think of them, those babies who vanished into the ether? Only rarely. I open the freezer several times a day and there's not a flicker of sadness. But there are moments out of nowhere that prick tiny pinholes into a sea of grief. Driving past the clinic where I stumbled out of the ultrasound room trying to hold it together until the bill was paid. Remembering all the pregnant women (whose turn was after mine) scanning my face intently for signs of life, and seeing instantly that there was none. I couldn't meet their eyes – they all knew anyway.

To all those childless women who so wanted to be mothers, I apologise for sounding greedy. I can only speak of what I know, and I knew number three was going to complete me and complete our family, and being a painfully tenacious person, I was not giving up. I wanted no regrets. Friends would say 'You'll know when you're done having babies'. I would nod and say 'maybe I am?'. But I knew I wasn't. So when the doctors told us that we had done almost everything we could to artificially encourage a pregnancy, we decided we had to walk away. Walk away and consult the pillow night after night about what mattered. In hindsight, it was my husband who realised my tunnel-vision had to end. Because it would come at the expense of the family we already had.

Those first few weeks of 'not' trying were like having no purpose. I needed a new obsession and I needed it fast. And it came just a month later in the shape of a cross on a pregnancy stick. A baby who knew her time had come. And who wanted me as her mother.

GENDER DIVIDE ALL MAN-MAID

My husband thinks a period drama is a movie about a woman with PMT. When he sees a petticoat and a china cup in the same television frame, he goes in search of the newspaper. By the time *Downton Abbey* finished its season, he was very well read and I was in mourning for Sunday nights, and the abrupt end to my well-to-do fantasies about living as landed gentry (mostly so I could have a maid). When I dabbed daintily at my tears after the hero lost his leg in the trenches (he found it later in the army hospital) my lord of the manor would look sideways at me from his newspaper, with lips as pursed as the dowager Maggie Smith.

Why can't men enjoy women's television? It always has stout-hearted blokes in it, what's not to like? Take *Downton Abbey*'s gilt-edged example: a manly aristocrat running his boundless estate, his wife, five daughters and a houseful of servants. Isn't that gentrified male fantasy too?: money, power, control, ladies-in-waiting? Or am I being common?

The gulf of good breeding between my beloved and me is widening as fast as a fallen woman in the family way. He thinks being confined to the Grand Prix for half a Sunday is all the drama anyone needs. Don't get me wrong – I love cars as much as the next woman (I had a buttercup-yellow Datsun 180B once) but I'll be blowed if I understand why staring at cars doing perpetual loops of a racetrack constitutes entertainment. I ask questions about which driver's doing what and why to stave off the boredom, but after ten minutes I am catatonic, even from pole position (closest to the telly).

And it's not just about who dominates the remote control. Domestic responsibilities are still unfairly divided along gender lines. I know this because our washing line has not been touched by a man since it was rigged up by one last century. Our washing basket lives undercover behind enemy lines – no-one but me knows it exists. It straddles the space in the laundry I call occupied territory – and there's no peace for me until it's empty. I don't know why my freshly ironed spouse thinks he can ignore all entreaties concerning washing, drying, folding and putting away the family's clothes, but my civil authority over this matter is clearly non-existent. (I now know encouraging people to put their smalls out is part of the delicate cycle of being a housewife.)

The dishwasher, however, is the landmine in our house. I love that appliance like no other—we know each other so intimately, I could fill and empty it blindfold. But my soft-skinned occasional kitchen-hand continually rearranges my bad packing 'for the good of the dishes'. I say it's a workhorse happy to get rough treatment, he replies that my cavalier attitude towards the art of plate stacking is beneath contempt. Late at night I hear him muttering under his breath as he restores efficiency and symmetry. It's just a pity he's not around to rearrange the two loads I've already done without him.

Domestic servitude is a dead-end job. We all hate it, we all want to do less of it, or share more of it. But it's a rare man who thinks about housework like women do. I know that because the latest census figures show a woman my age – a youthful forty-four – spends two hours and fifty-one minutes on housework a day compared to her mate, who puts in an hour and two minutes. (The two minutes is for procrastinating. Actually, maybe it's the hour that's for procrastinating?)

Lo and behold the census reveals that suddenly, at the age of eighty-five, Australian men get a taste for housework and out-clean their wives by eight minutes a day. The only possible explanation is that by eighty-five, a bloke probably feels he's held out long enough, or his wife has kicked the bucket waiting.

My live-in eye candy has become even more short sighted since I left my career on the box for life back in the nest. His clothes are now left where they've fallen, his coffee cups are plopped into the sink for the dish-hand and my morning vacuuming is an annoyance that interferes with radio news. He still mows a mean lawn, has the deft touch of a handyman and can get a squirming toddler dressed without tantrum, but I remain handmaiden to all.

But lately, an odd thing has happened. I seem to have risen above the resentment of feeling subordinate in my role as housewife, and have grown to tolerate the gentle hum of my morning rounds. While the breakfast chatter of children is at full throttle with dad, I quietly make beds with hospital corners and find homes for lost things. I think it's the need to control one's environment: my home is my office is my home. I still detest cleaning, but a veneer of household order is at least something achieved when writer's block strikes, or I discover that five-year-old has given two-year-old a sly haircut with the craft scissors.

Working mums have it much tougher. Many arrive home to the dreaded 'second shift'. After a full day on the job, they walk in the door to make a start on cooking, homework and baths. In-between they try to jam in some meaningful time with their children. If they're lucky, they have spouses who help to shoulder the load but plenty of partners are still toiling away in the office. Why has the division of domestic drudgery proved so resistant to change, despite ever-greater numbers of married women entering the workforce? Why are women still picking up the slack? Because most still aren't earning as much as men? Or because men would rather work late than come home to face a mountain of washing? No question – I'd rather stay holed up in the office as well.

I have sampled all the permutations of domestic life: I've been a double-income-no-kids, a working wife and mother of one, and a single mum trying to be all things to a three-year-old, pay a crushing mortgage and keep a level head at the office. Now I'm a mother of three with a breadwinner who allows me the luxury of a few precious years at home. Luxurious the hours may appear through the window of an office in town, but my day is no longer divided into work and rest – instead, I am always 'on' and 'doing'. I'm backed here by the latest statistics showing women get much less free time per day than men. No matter whether they work for money or love.

The biggest problem with domesticity is that it never ends, and no amount of technology has circumvented the tedium of keeping house. All I've learned is that the more housework a man does, the happier his partner is. And I'll hypothesise that men who willingly share the load get a lot less grief from the trouble-and-strife. In the meantime, I'll try not to care if my house gets trashed. I'll just remind myself that it's clean enough to be healthy, and dirty enough to be happy.

DEEP DOWN, IS MY MAN SHALLOW?

I live with a man who inhabits a different relationship to mine. Our marriage is a his-and-her version of the same conjugation. I can never tell what my husband is thinking because he's master of the poker face. On weekends, having tried (and failed) to read his mood, I'll squeeze in beside him on the sofa and inquire: 'Honey, what are you thinking?'

'Nothing.'

I like to press him further: 'You know, it's impossible to think about nothing. Even nothing is something if you can't think of anything.'

'Okay then', he sighs. 'I'm thinking about what a plonker that umpire is. And if I'll have time to scarper to Bunnings at half time. And whether they'll have a sausage sizzle out the front. Happy now?'

He shoots me a look that's either bemusement or incredulity but I can't tell because I can't read his mind.

I've spent years trying to get inside his head. I have tried to follow his man-mind by over-processing everything he says and does. I look for hidden meanings in his shrugs and read far too much into his harrumphs.

Here's my theory: my husband has a one-track mind. His brain chugs along the straightest possible route from A to B. He stays calm, measured and entirely predictable. As far as I can tell, he neatly divides his day into work, football, family, newspapers and sleep. (On weekends, he reverses the order.) And if the gentle hum of domestic life with a wife, three children and a cat turns into bedlam, he seeks refuge in the dunny.

On Saturday mornings, the bathroom floor is littered with newspapers. The sports section is in disarray, and the lift-outs have had pages torn out willy-nilly. No amount of my shuffling can get the paper back in page order. I can hear contented rustling as I walk past the john on my way to the laundry. The fan is a muffled roar. The kids are yelling for their dad to teach them table tennis.

I'm expected to respect his hide-out by declaring: 'Papa's ducked out to the shop to get milk!' And then I fumigate the hallway with lavender spray to throw them off the scent.

Why do I protect him from his own children? For love, apparently. What's a wife worth anyway? I've become as ever-present and useful to him as fresh air.

Sometimes, marriage and its chores are stultifying. For every man who dives for the dishcloth after dinner, there are plenty who push back their chair and announce: 'Delicious, darling.' Then they ignore the kitchen carnage and settle into the sofa to watch *Four Corners*.

It's never 50-50 in domestic work. It's 60-40 or 70-30. Or worse. One party works tirelessly to keep the household juggernaut rolling: the other enjoys the smooth ride.

Every six months or so I like to give our relationship a litmus test. I prop against the door of the study and casually inquire: 'So, honey, should we go out to dinner, just the two of us, and talk?'

'Talk about what?' he says.

'The state of our relationship.'

And he'll reply: 'It's chaotic. There. Now can we stay at home?'

It's the same answer every time. No man wants to talk about his relationship. Every woman likes to dissect hers.

My husband thinks my working week involves sitting around with my housewifey girlfriends drinking pots of tea and gasbagging. It's the kind of ignorant accusation that infuriates me and my two best pals when we meet on Friday mornings to discuss the rate of inflation and why our husbands are infuriating.

I admire those women who tell their man to shape up. Instead, I have a happy husband by default. I pretend I don't mind him always getting his own way because I don't want to sound like a nag. Instead, I only come unhinged every few weeks. The resentment backs up and explodes at inopportune moments. Usually on turbulent school mornings when he's swanning around after a twenty-minute sabbatical in the shower.

The sexes also divide over fine detail: I like a nicely made bed with hospital corners, my husband cuts corners by shutting the bedroom door. After dinner, he'll earn an adoring glance from me by announcing: 'Sit down Blossom, I'll do the dishes tonight.' And then he'll put the last four plates in the dishwasher and leave the crusty lasagne dish and a burnt saucepan on the sink.

Marriage is the accumulation of thousands of nondescript conversations held over thousands of unremarkable breakfasts. It's the kindness of a husband who lets me have the first shower, and the tolerance of a wife who picks up the five socks scattered across the bedroom floor. But next time the kids are screeching for their dad on a Saturday morning and I can't find the newspaper, I'm going to give them a wink and point them in the direction of the lavatory. I hope they annoy the crap out of him.

PAY YOUR MOODY DUES

Apparently PMS doesn't exist. Any woman claiming a monthly permit to grumpiness, gloominess and general wretchedness has had her licence revoked. Period.

So says a team of Canadian scientists who've decided Pre-Menstrual Syndrome is not a syndrome at all, but a convenient excuse for eighty per cent of the world's women to pay out on their partners once a month. Clearly those scientists haven't met my husband – a man who consistently gets my goat one week in four.

Just because Canadians invented the foghorn and peanut paste doesn't mean they understand women. I like to do the right thing and gift my man his independence during 'that time of the month': 'Feel free to say and do as you please honey, because this weekend I'm going to bite your head off regardless.'

So how did the best Canadian minds determine that women are faking their Preposterous Mood Swings every month? And why was the research team all women? (Because no man was brave enough to volunteer).

Based on a mere forty-one case studies, the scientists concluded that only six women could prove an emotional link between the end of their cycles and having more personalities than Glenn Close in *Fatal Attraction*. The other thirty-five respondents must have shredded their questionnaires in a fit of rage after their husbands left yet another Kleenex in a trouser pocket on washing day.

Canadian husbands must be agreeable all the time because I never hear of Canadian wives doing their block about a load of washing ruined by a blizzard of man-tissue.

Ever since I became a maidservant, I have been socially conditioned to blame PMS for doing my lolly once a month. I am sweet and docile by nature, but around the twenty-fourth of each month my husband goes from being a calm, considerate friend and partner to a demanding, unreasonable oaf. I give him my raised eyebrow of doom and growl: 'What did you say?' It's not because I didn't hear him, it's because I'm giving him three seconds to improve on what he said.

Really, women wouldn't need to manage their monthly anger if their partners could manage their stupidity. PMS was invented so women could have five days off from being nice to incompetents and idiots. Please don't take that week away from us!

The research team at the University of Toronto kindly left womankind with one sliver of credibility. It found women weren't imagining the *physical* symptoms of PMS: the cramps, the headaches, the bloating and the tiredness – they're legitimate – we can enjoy those. But now we can't blame hormones for any of the emotional baggage that piles up when our shop's shut for maintenance.

I'm sorry, I'm different. Twelve times a year, I speak three languages – English, sarcasm and profanity. When my bloke asks: 'What's up Blossom?' he can measure the speed and gruffness of my: 'Nothing!' to calculate just how much marital turbulence is heading his way.

My husband has the solution. He's inventing a mobile phone app that will warn him when I am about to become all three witches of Eastwick. It will plot my cycle and give him a heads-up one week out from impending domestic catastrophe. That's enough notice for him to plan a business trip out of town, or meetings to keep him working late in the office – any legitimate reason to be somewhere other than home. He's going to call his invention the Grief-O-Meter.

All men should consult their Grief-O-Meter before making plans with the wife for the week when pessimism is better than sex:

'Hey Blossom, let's go see that *Les Miserables* flick?'

'Nah, way too depressing.'

'Why? The plot? Social injustice? An impoverished woman ruined by prejudice who dies emaciated and alone?'

'Nah, a thin heroine.'

I say men are the missing ingredient in PMS – has anyone bothered to research whether the poor buggers actually *deserve* to be punished? My husband is not necessarily the innocent victim of a foul-tempered harridan who cries during cheesy Qantas ads.

Having an unusually calm and rational temperament, I am pushed over the edge by floors decorated with dirty socks and a man who turns the pages of his newspaper so loudly I can't hear Maggie Smith's acidic one-liners in *Downton Abbey*. Those Canadians may claim women have lost the excuse of PMS, but they've given us some much needed freedom. Now we can stop blaming our cycles and pinpoint the true cause of our anger – husbands.

I'm going to look on the bright side. If PMS no longer exists, then there's no need to confine my grumpiness to the last five days of the month. I can spread the grief around any time I like. How exciting! Next time you see me, best you give way to my broomstick.

CHILDHOOD ON THE HOOF

THE YOUNG, THE RESTLESS AND THE PLAYSTATION 3

Birthdays often end in tears in our house. Usually mine. That's how you know the party's been a good one. I've disintegrated from exhaustion.

But the last thing I expected was a birthday that *started* with tears. Two sleeps out from the big day, I sat my almost twelve-year-old down to deliver some unpleasant news: He was not going to become the owner of his much-coveted PlayStation 3, kingmaker amongst boys.

There was a moment's silence as the news sank in, but I was not prepared for the sudden wave of grief that swept over the dinner table and ran in rivulets through the peas and corn on his dinner plate. My son was crushed: 'I've been counting down the days, now no-one will ever come to my house again!' And he took himself off to bed puffy-eyed and inconsolable at 7.30 pm instead of 9 pm. (At least that was a nice change.)

He wasn't angry, just devastated. And I felt awful. I realised I had cost him currency in the playground. Already his peer group was jostling for elbow room, and exclusive membership required all the necessary gadgetry.

That night I wavered on my stance not to allow any teenage anaesthetic into our house: no PlayStation, no Xbox, no gaming consoles. My husband lent me enough of his testosterone to stiffen my resolve. By next morning, eldest child had bounced back and accepted his fate. His birthday was a triumph (and I didn't cry). In fact, with new headphones and a funky iPod cover, I overheard him telling a mate 'it was a cool birthday anyway'.

I'm afraid it was a hard lesson for me. As a mother, my nurturing instincts often tell me to clear the obstacles and smooth the road for my progeny, and here I was deliberately installing a speed hump. It got me thinking that maybe son number one felt he *deserved* a PlayStation and that his assumption had grown into hope, then into anticipation and finally into expectation, encouraged by my silence on the subject.

Perhaps the problem with kids today is their parents? My husband says I spoil mine. Spoil them how? With too much home cooking, lifts to school in the rain, unconditional love? Or does he mean spoiling them with new shoes every six months and a $20 haircut four times a year? Or rooms of their own and family holidays in rented beach houses?

Sociologists are reporting that today's parents will do anything to see their kids succeed. Why? For bragging rights? Or so they can be admired, or one better, envied, for having reared such high achievers?

'Never before have parents been so (mistakenly) convinced that their every move has a ripple effect into their children's future success.' So says Madeline Levine, a San Francisco psychologist specialising in young adults.

I see her point. I've been known to continue gluing and pasting a school papier-mache project long after my budding artist has lost interest. Are we prepared to stand back and allow our kids to fail, fall over and miss the bus? But am I one of those parents who can't say no? That's not me, I know that.

But perhaps I lean too far towards leniency. I give too many warnings and not enough punishments. I don't reward bad behaviour but I go overboard praising good. I try to be a spontaneous fun-loving mum rather than a cranky dragon. And that's the crux of it, isn't it – we're all *trying* to do a good job of raising our children? None of us is deliberately cocking it up. Often, all we have to go on is how our parents raised us and what we learn by osmosis from others.

My mum, in contrast, has the kind of authority over my children I wish I had. She's always consistent and her standards are demanding. All three of them love her fiercely and take turns behaving impeccably at her place. I watch, sometimes with awe, how she can head off an encroaching tantrum with quietness and patience until it dissolves into a fit of giggles. I can be clever like that too. But not after three months of crawling out of bed at 5 am to a juiced-up toddler, negotiating with a middle child who has made an art form out of crying wolf and managing a twelve-year-old who thinks he's twenty.

Life gets in the way of good parenting. I do my worst on school mornings, scrambled by the chaos of burning toast and missing socks, when shoes are calmly emptied of their sandpit on the lounge, and overdue permission slips are suddenly discovered at the bottom of bags. I rant and huff (apparently) and, on occasion, do my lolly.

Everywhere I go, I feel the watchful eyes of other parents, and nannas and grandpas, and worse, those not yet with children. Most of them look upon me with benevolence (and often amusement) but try disciplining a wayward two-year-old in the supermarket. I never know whether to feel proud of drawing the line, or ashamed of losing my cool. Usually I feel both.

Childhood on the Hoof

So are we as good at parenting as our folks were? Or better? Factor in the different challenges we face – children with endless choices and preoccupations: an overly connected world of play dates and catch ups, hockey practice, online gaming and text tag. There's no reason to be bored, yet I still hear the whines. I spent half my childhood on a bed reading, or building cubbies in untidy gardens or riding my bike tirelessly round and round the block. It was a simpler existence. Boredom made me creative.

Go back a third generation, that of our grandparents, and there were even more pressing concerns: would there be enough for a roast for Sunday lunch? Would they grow old enough to see their children into adulthood?

Maybe I'm in danger of being kiddie-whipped. I'm at home, doing endless housework, trying to write, and my five-year-old, drawing on the floor, says 'Can you bring me a yellow texta?'. I forget to say 'Sorry honey, I'm busy right now, you get it' and instead ask him to say 'Please?'

I know why I put the rubbish out and unpack the dishwasher. Because I gave those jobs to a twelve-year-old boy who left the lid open so often we had a plague of ants and who doesn't bother to check if the dishes he's putting away are still dirty. I can save enough time for an episode of *Desperate Housewives* just by doing it myself.

Hence the great conundrum of our serialised lives. We want to raise good people, who know the value of hard work, tenacity, generosity and kindness. But we're too quick to make it too easy for them, and perhaps they're leveraging that willingness and over-zealous investment. As one socially observant writer puts it: We've created 'a broad savannah of entitlement that we've watered, landscaped and hired gardeners to maintain', but we'd be better off 'letting the grasslands revert to forest'. (I've torn that out of *The New Yorker* magazine and stuck it on the fridge.)

For the good of my children then, I am going to let my house turn into the local dump. Beds will be lumpy and unmade, the cat will be starving and no-one will know where their clean uniforms are. I will stand back and allow my offspring to learn for themselves how to be on time for school and what really happens when they skip breakfast. And I'll lie back on the sofa and read the paper while I do my nails. Knowing I'm being a model mother.

THE BITE OF SPRING

I can smell spring in the air. The plane trees have burst into a canopy of lacy green shoots. After ten minutes in the sun I can feel it biting the back of my neck. I dig out the sunscreen from the bathroom cupboard. With my two urchins, we take our prized Manchester United soccer ball and head down to the park. (The ball was a Royal Show special – my six-year-old now fancies himself as the next Ronaldo.)

We slip off our shoes and gallop around on the grass. A wayward kick sends the ball rolling over a lush circle of green and we three take off after it, small daughter shouting over her shoulder: 'That was a rubbish shot, Mummy!' (She has all the class of a soccer hooligan.)

Our doughy winter feet thud over a patch of prickles, camouflaged by the soft clover: 'Yowwww!' Three-year-old freezes, then bursts into tears, unsure what has attacked her. Her left foot is a dartboard peppered with tiny spines. One by one I pull them out while she shrieks in my ear.

Six-year-old son hobbles towards me, also yelping. His pain threshold hovers around zero so I put him in a loving headlock and begin removing each prickle. (Competing against a squirming child, the maternal pincer grip is woefully inadequate.) At last, his foot is prickle-free. We limp for home,

Childhood on the Hoof

my own feet still stubbled with quills. Surely it's too early for blasted Bindii prickles? I can't believe there's been enough sun to harden the little blighters.

Bindii-eye weed has earned the collective hatred of generations of Australians: spiky land mines lying in wait for bare feet. As kids, we called it 'Jo-Jo.' We'd get our own back by crawling around the lawn on our hands and knees pulling up every juvenile weed we saw. We'd pinch out the still-green prickles and unravel their tightly coiled burrs, stringing them out in lines on the footpath. Then we'd stand back and admire the body count, satisfied that at least one patch of lawn would give us safe passage to the back door.

By January, any undiscovered Jo-Jo prickles had hardened their ability to inflict maximum pain. The baking sun turned the lawn dry and crispy by 10 am. A Jo-Jo spike could spear an eight-year-old's heel so flush to the skin that not even Mum's eyebrow tweezers could get a grip on the butt end. 'Go and rub your foot on the bricks' Mum'd say. I'd gingerly scrape my heel against the paving, hoping friction would dislodge the thorn. If it worked, the relief was instant. (Though like a Pavlovian dog, I'd already conditioned myself to walking on tiptoe.)

Other times, that spike in my heel would refuse to budge. Later that morning, I'd gently test my foot for the umpteenth time, applying my full weight to gauge the pain. There'd be a twinge, but I couldn't be sure if it was now an imaginary hurt and the prickle had left me hours ago.

Last week, I happened to be talking prickles with the bloke who owns our much-loved icecream bar. He remembers growing up in Geraldton when thongs came in black and brown and cost $2 at Woolies.

'We'd bolt into the house from the backyard and the only thing you'd hear was the 'crack, crack, crack' as the doublegees crunched into the lino as we walked. We'd take off our thongs and they'd be caked with the suckers. Big, nasty ones they were, like police road spikes – no matter which way they lay, one of those damn thorns pointed upwards. When a three-cornered jack got your foot, you'd show off the hole.'

Country doublegees were to town weeds what a king brown was to a gecko. When we were on summer holidays in Kalbarri, the locals would warn us: 'Watch out for that Tanner's curse – s'like a plague this year. It'll leave fork-holes in your soft city feet!' (I could only presume Mr Tanner was the bright spark who sailed into Fremantle from Capetown in 1830, thinking his doublegee plant might make a nice salad vegetable.)

Instead, doublegees took over. They stabbed bike tyres and clung on so you'd have to replace the tube. They jammed the blades of Uncle Andy's lawnmower and gave me new words to take to school: 'bloody bastards!' Doublegees lamed dogs, matted sheep's wool and contaminated grain harvests.

Standing chatting on the verge with our next-door neighbours at the weekend, I saw the wife was holding a bucket and a three-pronged gardening fork: 'Weeds wrecking the lawn already?' I asked.

'Jo-Jo' she replied, shaking her head.

'I know, our littlest one got her first foot-full down the park yesterday!'

'How'd she take it?' the husband asked.

'Oh, it was awful – she was howling and dancing around not knowing what was happening and getting more and more prickles.'

'The Rite of Spring ballet!' he laughed.
I hadn't thought of it that way.

THAT ELUSIVE STATE OF BLISS

Sleep deprivation is the torture of the damned. And I damn well can't put up with it anymore.

The smallest member of the house, now two, should be sleeping like a baby. Except that she never has, save for a brief and exquisite interlude last year. Now she collapses mute into her cot at lunchtime (a Mack truck couldn't wake her), only to spend the deepest recesses of night waking every couple of hours and crying long and loud for anything that might take one's fancy in the middle of the night – a hot bottle, a dummy, a cuddle, a rendition of the Wiggles at 3 am. It's infuriating and I am withered by tiredness.

I hope this will come with nods and hazy recollections from anyone who has ever had a child. Mothers and fathers and grandparents who look back on the halcyon days of baby-rearing and still see the black shadows of lost sleep.

I write this for those who have ever had problems with sleeping. Blokes of a certain age whose bladders have decided to start telling the time by nudging them awake every two hours. Women whose minds race ahead of their bodies, and whose brainwaves jolt them awake at five in the morning.

We take it so for granted, this third of our lives. It's supposed to be of fairy-tale proportions: still and long and dewy-faced in the morning. But Sleeping Beauty can be a right harridan – she's

Childhood on the Hoof

had it in for most of us at some time or other, and finding the magic kiss of sleep is often a brutal exercise in sheer bloody-minded frustration.

I'm sure, like me, you've tried all the usual trickery – no coffee, no television, a room as black as night, warm milk, a hot shower, a roll in the hay.

But if you're held hostage by a mind that won't relax and a body that refuses to drift, it can be the mother of all battles between id and ego. Never mind the superego – it's not playing by the rules either, and it has no conscience, happy to let you toss and turn mindlessly half the night.

A Harvard Medical School study documented that sleep deprivation causes the brain to become incapable of putting an emotional episode in the proper perspective. That would explain why getting on the scales makes me cry.

I hear from my mother and her friends that you need less sleep as you get older but it's all about the quality. That is, hours-in-a-row. They complain they can't sleep past 4.30 am or 5 am, and find it exasperating. Sleep deprivation at any age is the rack and thumbscrew of nightly torment, except the chambers now have electric blankets and duck-down pillows.

Most of what we know about sleep has only been learned in the past twenty-five years, since MRIs began giving us detailed images of the insides of our brains. In 2000, the biggest survey of Australian sleep habits ever conducted suggested women need an hour more sleep per night than men, and that not getting it may be one reason why women are more susceptible to depression. And that's depressing.

I thought I'd sail through the nightly interruptions of motherhood. After all, I'd had no trouble with the 4 am graveyard shifts in my early days in radio, the round-the-clock breaking stories and travelling to far-flung time zones only to have to hit the ground running. My camera crew and I prided ourselves on how, when it counted, we were machines, and could power our way through jetlag on next-to-no sleep. And then I had a baby.

I was very good at the four-hour shifts in hospital, and for the first few weeks at home, my post-partum brain bathed in the euphoria of a successful birth. I think adrenalin kept me going for a couple of months because the crash was as shattering as it was unexpected.

The only thing that was asleep for most of that first year was my legs. From sitting crumpled on the floor, one arm through the wooden slats of my baby's cot, mindlessly, endlessly patting his rear. Then came the aching back from rocking figure-of-eights and doing deep knee bends with a strapping ten-month-old whose head was lolling with sleep, but whose mother was too scared to put him down in case he wasn't asleep *enough*.

I was never going to make those mistakes with numbers two and three. Those babies were going to learn to sleep on their own, from day dot. No patting, no dummies, no rocking. That lasted until I got out of hospital. The tracksuit years, as we like to call them, were not kind. Nor was witching hour. I think the term is used to describe toddlers who hit the wall at 5 pm. In our house, it's when I do. And the lovely coven of my motherly friends know it's a bad spell that lasts a long, long time. Until the youngest of your brood learns how to do an all-nighter. And I don't mean party.

To test your mental strength to breaking point, try managing a crying baby and a sick child. Or get sick yourself. I see the drained, hollow faces most days on the school run – mums and dads you know have been up half the night. And their children, who despite such broken sleep, are still bouncing up and down. Until they get home again – for witching hour. Perhaps it is advancing age that ruins the delusions of parenting, that we all would have been better at it in our twenties, not in our thirties and forties.

My mother-in-law had seven babies in nine years and I have lamented to her of my altered state. She listened sympathetically and then said 'yes, mine all slept through from three months, at least I think they did – the door was shut'.

So last night I took her advice. I gave my two-year-old a little pep talk, a cuddle and a teddy. I turned off the baby monitor. I shut the door between her and us and I turned up the telly. Her father and I sat together on the sofa speechless. We listened to her cries and the hyperventilating that went with it, and stopped each other racing in to her to plant kisses on her wet cheeks. Eventually, after the longest twenty-five minutes of my recent life, she stopped crying. Completely. The silence was truly golden and eerily quiet.

We went to bed and celebrated. And then we took turns getting up every two hours when she cried louder and harder than she ever has.

IN SICKNESS AND IN GUILT

Being house-bound makes me queasy. So when our family of five was sidelined with gastro for thirty-six hours straight, I was positively bilious. No sooner did one of us emerge from the fug of sickness, than another would vanish into a darkened bedroom with bucket and towels.

That virus was so potent it took down grown man and small child with equal ease. But its curse was also a blessing, because that bug set me free from all domestic chores for an entire weekend. I did no cooking because no-one could stand the sight of food. I did no tidying up, no washing or folding because everyone else was too ill to care. But by Monday, I was post-viral and suffering a mother-load of guilt.

Here I was, ignoring the mounting pile of sweaty sheets and dry cracker crumbs, sitting cross-legged on the floor doing jigsaw puzzles with my youngest. She was the first to recover, and I was the only adult still functioning. We spent two hours threading buttons onto string necklaces and making cut-out paper daisies with her pinking shears. I loved our craft afternoon even more than she did.

And then I ruined my maternal pride by feeling guilty: guilty that I don't do this with her all the time. Why can't I ignore the dishes, the bills and the dirty floor and play Snakes

Childhood on the Hoof

and Ladders with my daughter? After all, I closed the door on my career to stay home with baby number three. I was the one who opted for a few precious years minding the nest. And yet I resent the endless loop of housework that now keeps me from my three-year-old.

The six hours between school drop-off and pick-up are the equivalent of a domestic nanosecond. That's why a dozen tea-chests are still waiting to be unpacked three months after we moved house. Meaningless chores like cleaning up the breakfast dishes and making beds take twice as long with a small helper and her funny little distractions.

Most mornings we traipse to the supermarket like explorers tracking the source of the Nile. We admire the bobcat machine three doors down as it loads house rubble into the tip truck. Then, as we cross the park, we begin our search for cockatoo feathers to add to our collection. Feather-hunting is thirsty work, so we stop for a drink at the tap and talk to the black pup who's licking up the splashes. The supermarket is still a sub-continent away. Some days I just want to nip to Coles and get bread and milk.

Am I being a carefree, accommodating mother, or a feckless, frazzled wife? Mums can't win: we overindulge our children, or we're too pushy. Or not pushy enough. We are suffocatingly present or dismissively absent.

Here's my stand on mother-guilt: I am not tirelessly dedicated to my children. In the midst of a screaming tantrum (theirs not mine), I view child-rearing as hard work and would escape to the office in an instant, if I had one.

Am I supposed to think of mothering as a gloriously female biological function? I did once, but that was before I had children. Now I lurch from one parenting no-no to the next.

Ranting is my latest imperfection. It turns relations between sleep-deprived mother and mouthy twelve-year-old into a powder keg. Sometimes, the unflappable father intervenes to restore peace and I get sent to the naughty corner: 'Blossom, settle down, go and take some deep breaths somewhere.'

I see classier mums and wish I could be more like them. Do they smile indulgently when their five-year-old eggs on his little sister to break open a packet of biscuits at the shops? I do my lolly in public and feel mortified. For that reason, I can enjoy watching other peoples' children behaving appallingly, because for once, they're not mine.

Do men feel father-guilt? The guilt of absence or indolence? In our house, the perfect dad weekend involves him sleeping, reading the papers and watching the footy. All done from the left arm of the sofa, with the kids using him as a trampoline to the next armchair. I don't think my husband feels any pressure to be anything other than what he is: a kind, fun and loving dad.

My mothering report card won't arrive until my children have craftily turned into adults. I hope they blank out those ugly school mornings. The ones when my fury curdled the milk on my eldest's Weetbix: 'What do you mean, that project is due today? What do you mean, you FORGOT?!'

Please let them remember how many *Women's Weekly* train cakes I laboured over, not the time I dumped their dinners in the bin when they whinged once too often about tuna pie.

I'd like to be remembered as the fun mum, the one who took them on pyjama walks in the dark, who rode the train just for kicks and didn't nag about unmade beds. I might be deluded, but I think back fondly to that awful gastro weekend, when in sickness, I did my best work.

SOME STARS TWINKLE, OTHERS SCORCH

Last week I had a disheartening conversation with a gaggle of schoolgirls in an ice-cream shop. My six-year-old son and his little sister were capitalising on the 'free taste tests' from an ice-cream lady who was tirelessly handing them morsel after morsel on tiny spoons. While two small children debated the merits of bubblegum over banana, I turned to the three teens behind us. 'Sorry! Are you in a hurry?' I asked. 'This is the most important decision my kids'll make all week. When I was an ice-cream scooper, we weren't allowed to give free tastes!'

The girls laughed and one replied: 'Like who'd ever work in an ice-cream shop?' I was taken aback. 'Yep', I said, 'the ice-cream was so hard, my arms would ache from dragging the scoop through it. I got paid six bucks an hour'. The girl in the middle snorted. I persevered: 'Have you girls got part-time jobs?'.

'Nah', they said, 'We're only thirteen'.

Curious, I asked: 'So any ideas about what you want to be yet?'

'Famous!' said the girl on giraffe legs, and for a moment I thought she was joking.

'Famous for what?'

She shrugged: 'Whatever. Just famous.'

On the walk home with my sticky children, I wondered if those teenagers believed fame was their birthright. Had they been brainwashed into thinking celebrity status comes without hard work?

Today the travelling circus we call reality TV sells us overnight successes. It thrusts people into the spotlight for brief applause then discards them as the parade moves on.

The last star I met was Bette Midler. In 1997, I interviewed her in Los Angeles. Her film *That Old Feeling* was about to premiere in Australia. It was a stinker and I expect she knew.

I walked into a posh hotel suite to find a woman with a huge head sitting on top of a pint-sized body. Her feet and hands were tiny – dainty extremities overwhelmed by a jutting bosom and a mop of frizz. She was sweating under a bank of studio lights that made her skin so dewy, I could barely make out where her face stopped and her neck began. Unaware that journalists should be lap-dogs during the Hollywood interview, I ploughed straight in and asked: 'Do you ever get tired of fame?'

She stared at me, then barked: 'Do you?!'

I spluttered something about being a nobody, but it was too late. She sulked for the next ten minutes. Refusing to make eye contact, she gave my questions one-syllable responses, not caring a jot about what Australian audiences would make of her. The interview was a disaster. The dressing-down tirade I got from her publicist afterwards was excruciating. I'm still not sure what riled her: my impertinent question or the fact she couldn't answer it.

I thought fame was unattainable when I was a kid. There were few celebrities in my patch of town, though a girl in my year had a dad who read sport on the TV news. That gave her instant social status at school. She had the kind of prestige that this single child of divorced parents could only fantasise about.

At age eleven, I would tear home on my bike to an empty house, knowing Simon Townsend's *Wonder World* was about to start. Our Thorn TV, on its sturdy wooden legs, needed a good ten seconds to warm up and deliver a flickering screen.

Sprawled into a brown corduroy beanbag, I was captivated by the most famous show on kid's telly. Simon Townsend was a reluctant celebrity. I remember reading in the newspaper that he'd been embarrassed when kids mobbed him at a school visit. I admired him even more for that.

Mum's rule was no telly after school, but my secret trysts with Simon Townsend made me desperate to become one of his roving reporters.

At puberty, the closest I came to hero-worship was plastering the walls of my bedroom with centrefolds of heart-throb Rob Lowe and posters of Abba. Celebrities were good wallpaper but their world didn't intersect with mine.

Now the likes of Kim Kardashian (famous for what, I can't remember) are slaves to their own publicity. Craving constant attention, they obsess as much about their following as the star-struck fans who stalk them on social media. The more bizarre the celebrity behaviour, the more the money rolls into their account.

I keep thinking about those girls in the ice-cream shop. They didn't want to become famous for being talented at something they loved. They were convinced stardom was a shortcut to wealth and happiness. But it was their sense of entitlement that puzzled me most.

I tell Mum about them and she remarks: 'In our day, if you behaved like a show pony, you were considered undignified. Famous people earned respect when they were humble.'

She was right.

I hate to say it Bette, but that day we met, you were obnoxious. I liked you better when you sang your way to the top.

THE HURT LOCKER: PASS THE MERCUROCHROME

I still have a big scar on my right knee from falling off the verandah at primary school. The drop from balustrade to bitumen was four feet but it felt like four storeys. Blood ran in rivulets down my shin as a crowd of girls in blue-checked dresses gathered round me in staring silence.

In sick bay, I sat on the edge of the starched white bed, jaw clenched, while the nurse picked out the gravel with her tweezers. She painted my gashed knee an even brighter shade of crimson with Mercurochrome. That stuff stains the memory of every graze and scrape from childhood.

Whatever happened to Mercurochrome? We always had a bottle in the cupboard. Didn't everyone? It might have contained mercury, but who took notice of labels back then? Mercurochrome was the only antiseptic that didn't sting like blazes.

I lived in my grandmother's house the year I turned eight. She wore pearls and drank Bovril and treated all my childish ailments with common sense: 'Only call the doctor when you need a stretcher.' Nan relied on a cupboard full of strange potions with exotic names and whiffy smells. The top shelf of her pantry was stacked with mysterious brown glass bottles, unguents, salves and liniments.

There was Savlon for her chilblains and milk of magnesia for indigestion. If one was stuck up, intestinally speaking, one took Carter's Little Liver pills (which played fast and loose and bypassed the liver altogether).

A plume of talcum powder followed in her wake after a shower. I was doused with it after mine. So much talc rained down on the bathroom floor that I would trace patterns in it with my fingers.

Nan believed in home-style remedies like Billy Graham believed in the Bible. I went to bed wearing her soft white driving gloves, tied firmly round my wrists with ribbon. Those gloves stopped me clawing at the eczema that itched uncontrollably in the creases behind my knees and my elbows. In the morning, it was my job to put Nan's gloves back on the dashboard of her Morris 1100, ready for the day's outing.

But her favourite tonic came in a tall, square bottle and was called Hypol. It was a fish-oil emulsion that reeked like a tin of sardines left out in the sun. She would pour out a greasy white glop of Hypol into a tablespoon, and I would hold my nose and force it down, trying not to gag. 'You won't get rickets after that', Nan would say, and then pour one for herself. 'Mmmm, delicious!' I could never tell if she was pulling my leg. (She also had a thing for Peck's fish paste on toast.)

Every few weeks she'd announce: 'This afternoon I'm going to the chiropodist to get my feet done.' I tried, and failed, to imagine what 'done' meant, but I didn't like the sound of it.

When I had a head cold, Nan would make me a tent out of a couple of towels and I would sit steaming my blocked nose over a basin of boiling water. It worked a treat. She soothed mozzie bites with calamine lotion and I trooped off to school covered in pink dots.

In the 1970s, Band-Aids were brown and fibrous and coated in industrial-strength adhesive. I'm sure they were designed to torment eight-year-old hypochondriacs. Mum would stride over as I lay soaking in the bath and declare: 'Rightey-ho, time that thing came off!'

In my panic I still had to choose: the slow torture of having the Band-Aid peeled off bit by bit, or the jolt of pain as Mum got a firm grip on the edge and tore it off. I would plead for the slow torture method. The Band-Aid, like a tick clinging to a dog, would refuse to lift. And then it dawned on me I was going to endure this persecution twice. 'Close your eyes!' she'd say, and the Band-Aid and I were ripped apart amid my shrieking. I used to cry that bit louder as Mum waved that wet parasite in a victory flourish; to me an extra dose of cruelty.

Now I patch my own children with Wiggles plasters that can barely hang on in a gust of wind. I watched a new Dettol ad on telly the other night. Some glamorous housewife was telling me that my children would catch the plague if I didn't douse every surface with disinfectant. I harrumphed in the style of my nan.

I remember boys at school would compete at enduring pain. They'd take turns to see who could poke themselves the hardest with a drawing pin. Or take bets on who could tolerate a Chinese burn the longest.

Are kids today just as tough? Just as resilient? I'd like to think they are. But if one of my brood came home pricked with drawing pins, I'm not sure if I'd reach for the aloe vera or ring the school psychologist. Perhaps it's me who has gone soft.

MY TRACK RECORD: SUCK IT UP, LOSER

It's athletics season. I know this because hurdles are sprouting from the soggy turf around school ovals. Long-jump sandpits are raked and crunchy with wet sand. I see girls with stilts for legs limbering up for the high jump. And I feel a wave of relief that my sports carnival days are behind me.

When I was a child, running races were an exercise in humiliation. I was gifted with neither speed nor endurance. At the crack of the starter's gun, I would jump in fright while the other kids charged out of the blocks. My swifter classmates would become a blur as they streaked away from me. I'd command my legs to accelerate, but already the gap between me and them was widening. By the halfway mark, my screaming lungs would overrule any fantasies about finishing in the top eight. I knew I was going to come a pink-and-flustered last. Again.

Up ahead, some kid with racehorse genes and a slipstream would feel the snap of the winner's tape and the pack would charge over the line as parents clapped and cheered. No-one needed to clock the time of the pig-tailed straggler, division six, making her lonely finish. Race officials were already pinning ribbons to scrawny chests barely out of breath. How I yearned to be fussed over in the winner's circle, to spend the day with a blue ribbon fluttering against my shirt.

Later, in high school, I tried out for the hurdles. I thought my years of trampolining might give me an edge at jumping and running combined. The hurdlers I'd seen were glorious to watch. They darted down the track like gazelles, gliding over the hurdles, each arc barely a blip in the silky rhythm of their stride.

And then it was my turn: I mowed down every hurdle but one, scraping the skin off my shin and wrenching my ankle.

'Now that's what I call a demolition derby!' My gym teacher patted my shoulder as I limped off to sick bay. Miss Wadsworth must have been pushing forty but she had the body of a greyhound and a knack for shattering egos: 'Stick with softball, hey?' she called, 'There's only eighteen metres between bases!'

Even now, I feel sorry for kids with no speed. I don't begrudge fast kids their glory, but it pains me to watch the losers: they look so dejected. I want to reach out to those little downcast faces and whisper: 'Coming first is over rated. It's how you handle coming last that counts.'

So I grew up to be a walker. Walkers think joggers should stay at home and run in a wheel – like hamsters – so we don't have to look at them. But they're everywhere in my suburb. The same beefy middle-aged man pounds past me as I stride up the hill to my local playing fields. I greet him with a jaunty 'Morning!' because I'm not struggling for air. Sometimes he'll grunt: 'Mornin' (no joyous exclamation mark). Other times he just jerks his chin in my direction because he's trying to hold back a heart attack. I hold my breath against his pungent sweet-sour smell and try not to stare at his contorted tomato-coloured face as he passes. But I think: 'No jogger ever looks happy!'

Childhood on the Hoof

The irony here is that, at forty-five, I've taken up running. I like to call it running because it makes me sound like an athlete. Now that I have my own tomato-face I can tell you why all joggers look pained: because they are.

Here's what I've discovered about middle-aged joggers since becoming one six weeks ago: running only becomes enjoyable when you turn into your street and you realise that in fifteen seconds, you will stumble through your gate. Then your lungs and your legs will finally stop hurting.

But last week, determined to experience a runner's high, I turned up at the playing fields where the super-mums do their hard-core training.

The super-mums introduced me to the trainer guy who we'd be paying to yell: 'Okay ladies! Off you go, across the oval, round the cricket nets and back.'

I took off across the grass, pumping my arms and urging on my legs until I could feel the headwind in my face and the dewy grass flattening under my hoofs. As I rounded the cricket nets it dawned on me that I had hit the front – the super-mums were at my heels, sprinting and talking at the same time.

I tore back towards the smug trainer guy, my chest burning, legs howling. As I reached him, he began to clap. 'Nice!' he yelled. I had won! WON! I bent double and panted violently (and euphorically) as the super-mums cantered in, still discussing their new-season bikinis.

And then smug trainer guy shouted: 'Righto ladies, that was your warm-up! Now for the sprints!'

I handed him a tenner, got into my car and drove home.

CORK CLOGS CRUEL MY 'COOL' QUOTIENT

You have to be cool to know cool. I have no such expertise. By the time I've noticed the trendy young mothers at school are wearing Birkenstock orthopaedic sandals, that foot fetish is over. My decision to shell out $130 for a pair of cork clogs is the tipping point that declares them passé.

Proudly wearing my new Birkies outside class, I spot several willowy mums having their tête-à-têtes in their new-season zebra-print ballet flats. I flinch, but this is nothing new. I have spent a lifetime trotting at the heels of trend-setters.

Of course by next summer, cork thongs will be 'in' again, but I'm a laggard. Cool people know when to deviate from the manual. I don't.

Over the years, I have tried to be cool. But the very act of trying is a guarantee of failure. Only once did I succeed – age twenty-six – by accident. After moving to Sydney in the middle of a steamy summer, I began taking long walks around my new city wearing ankle-grazing floral sundresses and Blundstone boots. I rode the crest of bohemian cool for an entire weekend.

I have often fantasised about parting a sea of admirers with my 'indefinable something', and hearing people whisper in my wake: 'Look at that! She's got it!' Instead, I clumsily part crowds with a stroller festooned with lumpish bags of groceries. My darting toddler has only two speeds: accelerating and flat out. My scooterised six-year-old gives chase, as pedestrians scatter for safety. Twelve-year-old son walks three paces behind, hoping no-one will guess he belongs to this vagabond family.

My eldest son and I used to be inseparable. He idolised me, and I was captivated by his boyish charms. Now he's like a boyfriend I've grown tired of, but feel obligated to keep. We have rare moments of the old magic, but mostly I can't remember what I saw in him. He now maintains a veneer of cheesed-off indifference, and I scrabble to keep him connected to the family flock.

I have tried pointing out to him that every generation thinks it's cooler than the one before. 'Yeah right!' he grunts. I've even suggested that he become a trailblazer at school by resurrecting the 1980s exclamation *Mint!* with his mates. I tell him: 'It's such a great word honey! It even *feels* cool saying it...*Mint!* And you know what? When everyone's saying *Mint!* you can start saying *Mintox!* That's for things beyond *Mint!*' He sighs and shakes his head: 'Yep Mum, that's a fully sick idea, one of your best.' Then he adds: 'Please don't come to Assembly this week. I can't stand the embarrassment.'

If I had street cred, everyone would want to talk like me and that would be *Mint!* Lacking street cred, I pretend to be hip on Facebook instead.

Social media has done cool people a disservice – it levels the playing field by allowing everyone to appear at their best. Facebook is an illusion – it encourages users to showcase only their prettiest, wittiest side. On Facebook, we can all be sophisticates posting our snappiest thoughts and most flattering photos. My cool friends say Facebook has had its day.

Childhood on the Hoof

And so has Twitter, says my fourteen-year-old god-daughter: 'Who does Twitter anymore?' she scowls, 'It's so, like, dumb.' Then she rolls her eyes at me: 'Don't you get it? When the mums start doing it, it's so, like – over.'

My book club, however, is still avant-garde after thirteen years. Twelve of us meet every six weeks to escape the twenty-seven offspring we have outputted since our club started. (We gave up reading the designated book years ago – *Bridget Jones' Diary* had become an annoying distraction to the more fascinating minutiae of each others' lives.)

In 2007, when I was pregnant, I discovered that one book-club girlfriend was on Twitter before I even knew what Twitter was. It sounded like a cult but I could tell it was cool. She could tell me fascinating insider stories about how Apple almost called the iPhone the TelePod. The only fascinating thing I could think to tell her was that I had a crush on my obstetrician. 'No way!' she said. 'Yes way!' I continued, 'And I think he's secretly in love with me too. When I'm on the examination table, he always catches my eye and smiles down at me through the gaps in the stirrups.' 'You dope', she said, 'He bats for the other side', and sashayed off to fill her glass. I felt decidedly uncool.

I've decided the essence of cool is indifference. And I am never indifferent. Instead, I made sure I married a man so laid back that at least my offspring have a fifty per cent chance of being cool. And if the gene pool fails them, I'll tell them to be proud of a mother who was uncool before uncool was cool.

THE PURSUIT OF HAPPINESS

THE ECSTASY OF ENTITLEMENT

What makes a contented life?

Almost everywhere I turn these days, I feel brainwashed into thinking I ought to be cheesed off with my lot. That I'm somehow entitled to a better life, that I deserve it because I'm worth it, L'Oréal-style.

We are living in the age of entitlement, where the expectations of a luxury existence have filtered down from the uber-rich to the people next door until even a couple of teenage newly-weds expect a home theatre and a two-car garage.

Am I so antiquated at forty-four that I can remember saving up for things? That I've finally learnt that more often than not, my needs are usually just wants? That my instant-gratification gene handed down through generations of women does not need to be instantly satiated? That waiting for the prize intensifies the pleasure of finally acquiring it?

It takes a concerted effort to examine our state of contentedness – we're so switched on these days, there's no pause button for reflection, no downtime. If you're not being pounded by emails and text messages, you're being earbashed by the phone. Surfing the internet means drowning in the bottomless deep of information and Facebook wants your wall papered with your every waking thought. No wonder our kids have trouble getting to sleep. The art of winding down after dinner with a good book or some music has been lost amongst the lounge room invaders of television and home movies and the ever-present news. (It takes a determined trigger finger to turn off the remote in our house.)

It's not until you go on holiday that you reacquaint yourself with the small pleasures of quietness, of not pushing into the corners of every silence with comment or conversation. You don't have to talk as much as you think. (Out loud. Or in the chambers of your mind.)

I blame the internet for blurring the boundaries between the haves and the have nots, for spreading at warp-speed the objects of desire until even my eleven-year-old takes for granted he's getting a PlayStation 3 for his twelfth birthday. (He isn't). With the big day approaching, I feel some trepidation at knowing his disappointment will be hard to assuage, and when all his friends have one, I don't blame him for feeling entitled to one as well. Unfortunately for him, his mother enjoys walking the tightrope of expectation and reward. And she thinks a PlayStation is an instrument for future malcontent. And to be quite frank, he and I don't need any more electronic sources of conflict.

I wonder if part of the problem is that for a good twenty years now, we've been constantly telling our kids they are special, and now they're living the label and won't have a bar of anyone who says otherwise. I hear stories of gen Y and the younger gen Xs, now in their twenties and thirties, expecting to climb their career ladders faster than anyone else, earn more than their mentors and oust their parents from their holiday houses on long weekends.

But does it make them happy knowing they are the most catered for generation in history? I doubt it. Perhaps all we've done is unwittingly create a breed of chronic malcontents, who can't stand criticism and disappointment, and whose overinflated egos can't handle the ugly realities of life. Like waiting until you're thirty to get a BMW. From your parents.

Am I sounding too harsh? Oh dear. I, too, tell my children they're extraordinary (usually in the cherished sense). But I've put the question of 'what makes a contented life' to a number of the more sensible members of our community – my mother's generation – who, in their late sixties and seventies, have their arthritic fingers firmly on the pulse of what really matters. And from those whose somewhat impending denouement gives them clarity of mind and memory, comes the slice of wisdom that the fierce work ethic of their day has been overtaken by the relentless pursuit of self-fulfilment.

Showing off your collected fixtures and fittings would have been bad manners in our grandparents' day. War and the depression, poverty, unemployment, rations and later the memories of it, left no room for discontent when luxuries were well out of reach. Perhaps then, happiness was as simple as a roast chicken on Sunday.

Today's epidemic of narcissism is being studied by a research team from Kennesaw State University in Georgia, which has been examining the results of an annual survey of high school students dating back to 1975. They have concluded that the younger generations want maximum income and maximum time off, two seemingly incompatible pursuits.

Surely one comes at the expense of the other? But trying to have it all is pointless and for most, it doesn't work. It just causes burnout. Not contentedness.

The older generation also knows the gift of self-sacrifice is undervalued these days. I think fewer young people today think of giving of themselves without expecting some reward in return. They don't call it the 'me' generation for nothing: blinded by the accumulation of material possessions, the outward trappings of a so-called successful life, it's about what's on show, not what's been achieved privately without public acknowledgement. I think giving something for nothing is a lovely recipe for content.

My better half gives me plenty of stick and gets nothing in return. Just my stony-faced silence. Which he quite likes (the silence part). He has a rule-of-relationships that you mustn't bicker over trifles, and you can't sulk about them either. You need to get your grievances out in one hit, without shouting, agree with his point of view, apologise for yours and move on. He is infuriating but one of the most contented people I have ever met. Is he onto something? Not sweating the small stuff and always being right? I try in vain.

Sometimes, when the dishes aren't pressing, and dinner is in the oven, I sit outside and watch my children at play. In that brief window before teatime when they're happily going about their business with a watering can or two rocks and a leaf, I feel content. Content with the healthy little family I have produced; content that I am able to stop still and watch a fleeting vignette of childhood, content that they are absentmindedly content.

And then drifting over the smell of roses comes the smell of burning casserole, and I awake from my Madonna-and-child torpor to the reality of domestic discontentedness. It pierces the air with its high-pitched shrieks of sibling rivalry as middle child yells 'What's for dinner?'. And I proudly yell back that I've cooked a beef bourguignon to remind us all of our once-in-a-lifetime trip to France in 2012. And he looks at me and says 'ugh'. Content indeed.

WHO GIVES A FIG FOR OUR FAMILY TREE?

How wonderful to find a fig tree growing wild, the tips of its branches sagging under the weight of dozens of fat purple figs.

Sixty-six years ago my mum discovered a giant fig tree jutting out from the banks of the Swan River. To reach its uppermost branches where the ripest figs were sunning themselves, she would climb barefoot up the rocky cliff and shimmy out along the sturdiest branches. She could only pick as many as she could hold in one hand without falling off her perch. And there she would sit, scarlet juice running down her chin while her brother shouted up from the beach: 'Drop some down to me Sis! C'mon! It's not fair!' (A fear of heights and pianist's hands meant climbing trees was not his forte.)

My mum likes to think of that particular tree as 'hers'. It has stood beside three generations of her family, tolerating the multi-million dollar mansions that have sprung up around it. No-one has dared fire up a chainsaw despite that tree hogging the best of waterfront views. Every year my mother makes a pilgrimage, green bucket in hand, to 'her' tree. She won't tell fig-loving friends where it is, and her secrecy has become a running joke: 'Hey Joanie, have you put the coordinates of that tree in your will yet?' Most years her clandestine operation is sabotaged, not by informers, but by the dozens of ringneck parrots that get a toe-hold in the canopy before she does and gorge themselves on the best fruit.

My mother's lust for wild figs is as curious as her unorthodox manner of eating them. She tears the fig in half and mashes the two pieces together until the red flesh spills over the skin and she eats the resulting mess in raptures. (I don't understand why either.)

Every summer I look forward to the day Mum calls to say: 'Time we went down to my tree', and the kids and I pile into the car: 'Fig-hunt!'

Expeditions to that secluded bend in the river have become a rite of passage in our family. Members are allocated their responsibilities according to sprightliness and fervour. The little ones are the 'fig spotters', the more agile are 'climbers' and those who'd rather man the bucket are 'catchers'.

My normally rebellious twelve-year-old revels in the best climbing adventure of the year. He yells down through the branches: 'Hey Nan, there are loads up here!' It's a rare thing for a child born this century to share a slice of his grandmother's Huck Finn heritage, still there for the taking. Summers have come and gone but the big brown jellyfish still beach themselves on the river's edge, and the water in February is always briny and warm. We now carry a plastic bucket instead of a tin pail. The older I get, the more determined I am to keep this ceremony alive. I picture myself as a doting nanna telling my grandkids not to worry when the milky sap from the fig-stalks itches their skin: 'It's not poisonous poppet. Have a dip in the river and you'll be right as rain'.

I want to impress on my children the value of belonging. I want each of them imprinted with this family ritual for when they need to remember where they came from. I savour that a new generation of sturdy little bodies is just as adept at finding treasure in the tree.

After an hour by the river, Mum's bucket contains enough figs for a dozen jars of jam and chutney but the branches are still laden. She and I like to amuse ourselves by having alibis at the ready for the odd dog-walker who wanders past: 'Did you see the possum up there?' Mum looks forward to the day she can stand her ground before an inquisitor and declare: 'The tree's mine. I planted it.' (Exaggeration is a dominant gene in our family.)

Mum's tree, of course, is everyone's tree. Like the huge mulberry we found as kids when the house up the road got demolished and the backyard was indecently exposed. On Sunday afternoons, half the neighbourhood kids were stained crimson and we were too full of juice to eat tea. Back then, every house had a loquat or a plum or an almond tree, a passionfruit or a muscatel grape. Harvests were shared around for jams and preserves and came back in recycled pickle jars wearing gingham hats cut with pinking shears. Rear laneways were common ground for cricket games and cubbies and family histories intertwined over side fences like the tendrils of vines reaching for new strongholds.

My wish is for my mother's secret tree to still be there when my children have slyly turned into adults. When their childhoods can be recaptured in an instant by that bark under their feet or the coarse leaves in their hands. The tree won't look as big to them as it once did. But I hope it will loom large when they reminisce about the innocent adventures of a bunch of kids and their prowess as a clan.

SEND FOR THE DOCTOR THIS AFTERNOON

What is it about growing up in Perth that sticks to me like beach sand whipped up by the Freo doctor? Remembering mums and dads struggling to wrap wet kids in flapping towels. Brothers and sisters duck-diving under waves trying to stall their departure until someone shouts over the howling wind: 'Ice-creams for kids who help carry!' Everyone searching for their thongs.

Try explaining to someone who's not a native: 'Hey! I think the doctor's in' – that bastard-saint of bluster and balm so familiar to Perth beachgoers. The sea breeze that's welcome relief from yet another stinking hot day, but the killjoy that makes the beach so unpleasant everyone packs up and heads back to the baking car. As a kid, the bitumen was always so hot you had to stand on your towel until there was a break in the traffic. Back then, as we drove away from the sinking sun with all the windows open, I would take one last look back at the ocean, sun-dappled but choppy now. One last laugh at the seagulls being buffeted sideways as they swooped down to the fish-and-chips wrappers on the grass.

Thirty years later, these are the memories that hallmark an Australian childhood. We must tell our children how we tortured the Hills Hoist in the backyard, how it made terrible creaks and groans that brought Mum outside to tell us off. We, too, now have the buffalo lawn, and another generation of kids knows the sting of grass cuts from rolling around on it. Someone still gets sent inside to fetch the calamine lotion. And little ones still go to bed in shortie pyjamas with the fan on full bore, legs covered in pink calamine dots.

I want my children to know by instinct all these ways of being Australian. I want to hear them squeal as they jump on the trampoline while Papa squirts them with the hose. I want them to know that the best thirst quencher is a slab of cold watermelon; that the hot plate needs a slosh of beer before you cook a dozen snags. I think back to all those backyard barbies where Uncle Hughie would send me inside for the tomato sauce ('Get the dead horse for me will ya Rosi-gal!') I would sit by his elbow and marvel as he drowned his steak in it.

Killing flies was small-game hunting when Mum handed us the red plastic swatters she kept on top of the fridge. (Fly spray was expensive and only for special occasions.) Anyone who didn't shut the flyscreen door got a peeved: 'Were you born in a tent?!'

I'd spend Sunday afternoons on the swings at the park with a girlfriend from six houses up. Sometimes we'd vanish to the corner deli to play pinball while we waited for *Countdown* to start. We'd blow our pocket money in an hour, but a dollar lasted for ages and Smarties were three for a cent.

I try to give my twelve-year-old son the same long leash – let him skateboard round the streets and vanish 'up the shops' with a mate. I hope he's sensible enough not to take for granted the freedoms I give him, because I feel uneasy every time I let him out the door. At the same age, I was horsing around at the local pool for hours, only coming home when I was hungry.

I spent most Saturday afternoons unsupervised at the tennis club, racing my blue bike up and down the driveway, or hitting balls up against the clubhouse wall. The members' last sets always seemed the longest – waiting around for the grown-ups to finish play because then we were allowed a packet of chips and a bottle of red creaming soda. With a paper straw. We didn't get in the way of the adults socialising: we were part of a family, not the centre of attention.

All those sunburns, and heat rashes, and chafing from too much sand in our bathers – the small but vivid discomforts of an Australian summer. How many times did I slather myself in baby oil and lie out in the backyard to summons the New Year's tan? That night, I'd be soaking in a bath loaded with bicarb soda to take the sting out of red shoulders. My children's peachy skins will be saved by sunscreen and long-sleeved rashies. And the comfort of air-conditioning.

I have promised my children we will go to the beach every single day of the summer holidays. Their father thinks that's way too much effort. But I have chosen to ignore the sand-pit in the car and the endless wet towels. Rather, the kids and I are now craving our daily dose of sea and salt. With each swim, a new generation of Aussies is laying down a patina of beachside memories. I hope these memories will be easily retrieved when, in years to come, someone asks them: 'So what was it like growing up in Perth?' Or better still: 'Who's this Freo Doctor?'

THE SOUNDS OF SILENCE

When was the last time you heard silence? Not the soothing emptiness of the countryside, with its carolling magpies and leaf-rustling breezes, but the complete absence of sound?

I've experienced true silence just the once, suspended in the watery blackness of a float tank in Sydney. Climbing naked into an isolation chamber with nothing for company but lukewarm salty water is an exercise in sensory deprivation.

It was a gag – a gift voucher from my mum wanting to slow me down. I was only thirty, but I still remember the mesmerising stillness that sent my brain darting about in bewilderment, straining for input. (There are only two choices in the confines of a float tank: give in to the nothingness, or have an anxiety attack.) I could repress the urge to panic knowing I could escape the tank, but emptying my head of noisy thought was the biggest challenge. Concentrating on the sensations of breathing loosened my grip on time and I emerged an hour later in a state of dreamy calm.

I've never again come that close to silence. I've tried to find it lying in the yellow stubble of the furthest paddock at the family farm, but the pulsating chorus of cicadas became intrusive, underscored by the thundering of a road train from across the valley. Last October, being laid out on the white slab of a medical imaging suite became the best manufactured silence of the year. I needed a forty-five minute bone scan on my foot. Forbidden to move a muscle, I drifted into a trance, spellbound by the gentle purring of the machine. If not for the $500 bill, I'd be tempted to book in again – just for the afternoon nap.

Silence and modern life now seem incompatible. There is supposedly not a single place in Europe where you can sit still for fifteen minutes during daylight and escape the noises of mankind. That's quite an assertion. Whether the truth or exaggeration, we humans have burdened the planet with the incessant racket of our machines.

As I write, it's night-time and I am sitting at my desk with the sash windows open. The kids are out to it after a late swim at the beach. Their father is in Manila on business. (When people ask what he does up there, I say: 'He collects folders.')

It's tranquil, but still saturated with sound. If I tune my ears, I can hear the faint whirring of the ceiling fan in the kitchen creating an evening breeze. There is a glee club of frogs in the garden celebrating Retic Day. My fingers do a sibilant dance over the keyboard. A car turns out of our street and revs into high gear. Someone laughs next door. With my eyes closed I can detect the low drone of the fridge and a pulsating sensation in my head. A wave of relaxation washes over me, replacing the effort of listening.

I spend much of my time living outside of myself. If I'm not moderating the squabbles between my children, or trying to have three conversations at once, I'm straining to hear the TV news as I bang about in the kitchen cooking dinner. A dozen things always demand my ears. Even when my body is still, I continue to cartwheel round the inside of my head: racing ahead to tomorrow's conundrums or fretting over yesterday's. I've heard it called 'the storm of inward thought.' I'd prefer to be becalmed.

My favourite time is those minutes before I fall asleep, when the house is softly breathing, and I'm alone with my thoughts. I bring them before the Bench to be counselled, deliberated and settled, and then I wind down in the deep quiet.

Remember the silence of the classroom when you were at high school? Me neither. But I do recall brief lulls in the chatter when we kids finally knuckled down and the only sound was the scratch of biros on paper. It was stimulated silence: minds on the stretch, neurons firing. (Or, in my case, neurons scattering in confusion during maths.)

Silence is satisfying. Advancing age has given my mum an intolerance for the bedlam of my house. When three kids are banging doors, shrieking and galloping around their nanna, and the thumping music on eldest son's radio is competing with our conversation, I can see her becoming agitated.

Before long, she's kissing the kids and searching for her car keys to escape my noisy world. One child at a time is my answer for Mum, especially with a two-year-old who has only two volumes – shouting and yelling.

I've made it my goal this year to seek more silence. I need some tranquilising. While my toddler is napping, I'll try to create a mind-space so soft and still I'll be able to hear a pin drop. With cork floors here, that should be quite the challenge.

GOOD DEEDS SHINE IN A NAUGHTY WORLD

The kindness of strangers is never wasted on me. Especially when I'm naive enough to believe small children can be good in a sofa shop after a lemonade icy-pole. It wasn't the sticky hands or clothes that was the problem – I'd mopped up and they were spotless and un-sticky. Perhaps I underestimated the sugar-rush, but they were already euphoric from a swim at the local pool.

This was a day when two strangers showed me their capacity for tolerance and good humour. My children, who had been giggling hysterically in the car, wanted to go to the park. Instead, I took them to an expensive leather furniture playground.

It started out well. They were rolling around in a shag pile rug as though it were long grass. (Price: $1,799, on sale.) They chose a replica Eames armchair each, counted to ten and madly swapped seats. (Price: $1,950. Each.)

Then while I was flipping through the fabric samples (inwardly cursing the prices) with the immaculately groomed sales lady, my two-year-old decided to strip off her nappy and dress and leap all over a white leather sofa in the buff. (Sale price: $4,050.) Her brother, impressed, threw off his shirt and shoes and ran half a lap of the cavernous showroom shrieking for his sister to chase him.

I made a mental note of the exits and then met the sales lady's eye: 'I'm so sorry, they've gone completely mad. Give me one second to round them up and we'll be out of here.' Without a hint of annoyance, she said: 'Oh they're fine, this is floor stock you know – you're allowed to try out the furniture.' I could have kissed her.

With quote in hand, and daughter reacquainted with nappy, I decided to tempt fate by calling in at a gourmet supermarket on the way home. Already, toddler daughter was tired, and small boy was coming undone. This time, they really cut loose.

At the deli counter they went to town on the free olives on toothpicks until I lifted the whole tray out of reach and stood there like an idiot waiting for some staff member to relieve me of it.

Next my daughter decided to stack the sausages in the open fridge into towers while five-year-old attempted chin-ups on the butcher's rail. In the middle of this circus, I was trying to order mince for meatballs. And all the while, I was grabbing for one rascal's arm as he whisked past me on the way to the free crackers, while I tried to convince his sister to ride in the trolley so I could manacle her to it.

A couple of bystanders awaited the results as I warned my children: 'This is your last chance, I'm counting to three!' I got to three (and even tried 'Four!') but the rampage continued. I moved up a gear and threatened to withdraw all future ice-creams after swimming lessons: 'No, Mum no!' That seemed to work quite nicely.

Out of the corner of my eye, I saw an older woman approaching me and mentally prepared for a dressing down. She stopped and leaned in so no-one else could hear: 'You're doing a sterling job of disciplining those little monkeys. I'm a teacher of thirty years and I know a good mum when I see one. You're going to get lovely adults out of them one day.'

I was astonished. I didn't know what to say, so I told her the truth: 'I thought you were going to give me a lecture about my terrible parenting – the kids are completely nuts today and the third one's not even here!' She patted me on the shoulder: 'Enjoy, you're doing fine.' Then she was gone.

All day I thought about those two women. Two strangers who had given my desperate mothering their stamp of approval. In one hour, those two ladies did more for my self-esteem than all the parenting books I've slaved over.

Most days I question my child-rearing abilities and they come up short. Am I spoiling the little one by bribing her with a jellybean for every wee in the toilet? How hard should I come down on the big one? His twelve-year-old insolence would have earned me the whack of the wooden spoon when I was his age. Am I strict enough for society's liking? Do I care too much what other people think?

With stares and frowns, society likes to judge women on their mothering, but rarely have I seen a dad chastised in public for his fathering. I notice people act indulgently towards dads and unruly kids. They're off limits, earning credits for effort. Mothers are fair game. Why? When I see a tantrum in the lolly aisle at the supermarket I give the mum a wink and grin: 'Having fun yet?' just so she knows I'm on her side.

Perhaps that's why a stranger's acceptance and encouragement is such an unexpected gift. Even more reason to say to two women who clearly remembered the trials of motherhood: thank you.

LIFE: INTERRUPTED

WHEN A FRIEND DIES YOUNG

Life, interrupted: in hospitals, you find all the lonely people. Where do they all belong?

I've been spending a lot of time in a public hospital lately, visiting the dearest of girlfriends. She is no stranger to chronic illness, but this time she scared us. Out of immediate danger, she now lies in a room pasted with photos of her small angel-haired son as streams of visitors take turns keeping vigil by her bedside.

I'm one of those people, urging her on, whispering fighting words in her ear, silently cursing an illness so fierce it chose at whim to blacken five days of her life with a coma. On the long walk from the carpark, I have become acutely aware of the divide between well and sick — I feel almost guilty, not grateful, to be in rude health with no reason for marking time. Twice now, I have passed the same elderly man huddled at the bus stop. I can't tell if he is wishing the bus would come, or just thankful for a place to sit, protected from the wind. He looks worn down by the business of living, weary of his age. How does he come to be here? Is there someone waiting for him somewhere?

All along the corridors of Ward 71, left and right, doors ajar, I see glimpses of lives visited by sickness. The signs of infirmity are everywhere: the musty air and the strange medical smells, the half-light, windows with a view of more windows, all shut to the outside world. The only energy I feel is from the nurses, so cheerful there is no small comfort too big to ask them for – the place enlivened with their briskness and busyness.

Squeezing in behind a gurney in the giant lift, I'm given a close-up of someone wrapped in a white blanket: a middle-aged man too unwell to care if I see him at his most vulnerable, at his lowest ebb. The orderly smiles at me across his parcel: for him, moving between floors with a patient on a trolley is part of the ups and downs of an ordinary day. For me, it's like stepping into another dimension, the underbelly of the human condition. A half-life of bedpans and hacking coughs and pressure stockings. Another world we all acknowledge, but vainly hope never to enter.

Nothing reminds you of your good health more than seeing someone without theirs. Even small tastes of illness signpost how the spirit can falter when sick. Unless you're Clive James, terminal with leukaemia (and recently kicked out of home for infidelity), telling a journalist: 'In my life I have managed to get a certain amount done, and my chief aim now is to live longer so that I can do more.' Usually, fear of the unknown is the default position when ill health announces itself, until doctors reassure us modern medicine will save us. Or at least give us reasonable odds. Then it's down to mental grit: can we overrule a mind that threatens to run wild with doubts and panic, that carries us off down dark, gloomy alleys morbidly pointing out the dead ends. Conquer that subconscious traitor and you're on the road to recovery.

I have been desperately sick only once, eight days after my third baby was born. A post-partum haemorrhage that threatened to be my undoing, just as I'd completed the miracle work of giving birth. Not once during that twelve-hour ordeal, with teams of doctors swapping shifts through the night, and the father of my week-old baby left to his own devices behind the throng of white coats and soft-soled shoes, did I ever let myself believe I would leave my family. But I saw the looks on the faces of the emergency team, as they smiled down at me and squeezed my hand, and gave each other those lingering glances that meant I was in real trouble.

I never considered I might die – I had my new baby fretting in the hospital nursery for her mother's smell and touch. There were two young boys whose lives would falter without their mum. And a husband who hadn't planned on raising his family alone.

I have rarely thought about that time until now, weaving my way along hospital corridors to the bedside of my friend. My lovely friend, who has known no end of sickness by (ill) virtue of the awful junction between her genetics and advancing age. On she fights, frail now, but robust enough of mind to know she too, is needed by many.

Through it all, there are the constant reminders of what she can no longer do or be – that bastard disease hungry for the healthy parts of her. Doctors, one after the other, testing their own limits to rebuild a body under siege, trying to reverse the damage already done with ever more arcane treatments. And what of the girl I grew up with, in and out of hospitals her whole adult life, now mother to a six-year-old, confined to a bed yet again? Where is her freedom to just 'be' – her independence curtailed by the nemesis inside her, and on the outside, by those whose job it is to save her with endless tests and doctoring.

Life: Interrupted

What can illness teach us? We can fantasise about endlessness, knowing full well the end will come to all of us. But often the transformation from person to patient is insidious. Our lives suddenly on hold as the enemy infiltrates our defences and takes away our control.

I have known those who regard their sickness as a companion, no friend but also no foe. An unwanted possession to be outgrown, outwitted and outlived. The American essayist Susan Sontag wrote that: 'Illness is the night side of life, a more onerous citizenship. Everyone who is born holds dual citizenship, in the kingdom of the well and in the kingdom of the sick. Although we all prefer to use the good passport, sooner or later each of us is obliged, at least for a spell, to identify ourselves as citizens of that other place.'

What of the old woman in the room next to my friend, residing in 'that other place?'. Just a small face above the sheet, always alone, her wispy white hair a tangled halo on the pillow. Where are her visitors? Are there children or a husband to love? She looks peaceful when asleep, as she mostly is when I pass by. I wonder if she will ever leave this place, with its ticking machines and constant footsteps, for the peace of her own home, wherever that might be? Will there be some other freshly made bed, comforting and familiar from which to recover from her sickness?

George Bernard Shaw once said 'I enjoy convalescence. It's the part that makes the illness worthwhile'. For my childhood friend, the convalescences get longer and more torturous, small parts of her lost along the way. How long will her recovery take this time? How much more damage will be done?

Feeling utterly useless, I will use my sturdy health to replenish hers; even if I can do nothing more than breathe the same air in a stuffy room screened by a blue curtain. I'll take her my children's drawings and let her see herself as a stick figure in a glittery dress with a crooked smile. And I'll whisper the story of an old man huddled at the bus stop who was rewarded at last, when an old friend pulled up in a car to take him home.

THE COLLATERAL DAMAGE OF DIVORCE

Reconciled with daughter Ros after abandoning her as a toddler, Tony Thomas shares her column to mark Father's Day. They agreed to write each other a letter about their separation, and to open and read them simultaneously. They hope their stories will resonate with other fractured families.

Lament for fatherhood lost
Ros Thomas:

A great gulf of loneliness stands between me and my father. And it comes from not knowing. Not knowing who he is, or which parts of me are him. Of not knowing his face and voice by heart. I often catch myself watching my children and their besotted father at their funny games, reliving my childhood vicariously through them. Wistful thinking. I never had a dad. He is a mythical creature in my life.

There is not a single photo of the two of us together. No teary pride with newborn bundle in the delivery suite. No small-girl shoulder rides. Nowhere high from where to view the world.

Actually, there was one dog-eared snap of us, lost now, but it was only of his hand steadying mine as a laughing toddler in the bath. (I held that photo so many times as a kid; I thought if I looked hard enough, I would see love in that hand.)

It never really mattered to me as a child. My mum was my whole world. But there were always the awkward moments at other people's houses when someone would ask 'Where's your dad?' and I would have to answer stupidly 'I don't know'. By the look on my face, they wouldn't push further.

There were the odd fleeting visits from him, a strange man at the door, whisking me away to an unfamiliar house with new smells and foreign voices. Another family that was mine, but with no history for either of us. Studying his face for reflections of my own and finding none. A terrible sense of disconnectedness. The loaded silence on the drive home. An awkward kiss on the cheek on the way out the car door. Floods of tears once safely inside.

Funnily enough, I never pined for him on birthdays or at Christmas, there was always too much other excitement. I don't think I ever looked at friends' fathers with awe or envy either. I just wanted one of my own. A keepsake.

It was the quiet times, playing alone, when I reflected begrudgingly on how different I thought I was, and why it had to be me who had a half missing.

By high school it was my great shame. A reason to feel somehow inferior in the crowd. When the stigma of divorce was an impediment to fitting in. I hated him for it.

By the time I was interested in boys, I already had a thing for men. I was a walking stereotype. There were lovely boyfriends with fatherly kindnesses and affections, but they were somehow too simple. I needed the angst-filled, heaving burden of unrequited love. I found it at university in the great novels

I studied and buried myself deep in Oedipus and Electra and became as father-fixated as ever.

How many other fatherless children are out there? How do we reconcile the disappointment of growing up feeling tainted by absent dads, or present ones who can't live up to their responsibilities? Or expectations? Maybe they thought we'd be better off? Maybe we were. And how do we make a happy life for ourselves despite rough starts? Blame won't help. Nor will anger. Or casting yourself as victim. I decided to take the part of heroine instead and strained to live up to it.

Now in my forties and a mother, my great hurdle is how to break the cycle of abandonment that is now two generations in the making, and was very nearly a third. I feel intense, sometimes overwhelming pressure to ensure my second marriage is a happy union of parenthood and compatibility. Because I cannot fail at delivering my children the unconditional presence of a father.

As a late bloomer, one who didn't really hit her stride until her mid-twenties, I have reconciled myself as the abandoned child made good, saved by the love of a mother and later, husband, friends and children. And I now recognise, and more importantly embrace in myself, the fears and self-doubts of a fatherless daughter. For few of us are gifted the perfect childhood.

Mea culpa for the sins of the dad who wasn't there
Tony Thomas:

My father returned from the war to find himself supplanted. He flew to Brisbane, for good. The drone of any plane had me rushing out to wave him a six-year-old's welcome home. Who would think, after that, that I too would fail as a father? I reported for *The West Australian* for twelve years. Ros, you were three when I left my marriage and job in 1970 for Melbourne and then the Canberra press gallery. This was for my own good, not yours. On my last night at home, I sat and watched you for hours, asleep in your cot. I marvelled that I could be so selfish.

The following year was the turmoil of marriage separation and break-up and a new wife and plenty of career stress. About a third of my then-modest pay went on maintenance payments to Perth. I could just afford to build a house in Canberra. It was Struggle Street for both estranged families.

I seldom flew back to Perth for access. What is a father meant to do on an afternoon with a daughter who is now a stranger? There is only 'activity'. One time we ran around happily, both of us at eight-year-old level. But as you got older, visits became clumsy affairs. After one visit, I howled with grief.

Each gap seemed to lead to a longer gap. When you were about fourteen, you wrote me a newsy letter about your life and your dog. It was a chance to start building bridges but nothing came of it.

My second marriage had also failed and this time, now in Melbourne, I was determined that I wouldn't lose my son and daughter in Canberra. This issue involved counsellors, barristers and a court. I kept up fatherhood, at least with my toddler son.

But I didn't have emotional energy left for an uphill campaign to generate a fatherly relationship with an adolescent daughter in Perth, who I assumed was busy sorting out local issues.

Maintenance to Perth became less onerous through wage inflation. It is sad that this outflow was the only nexus between our two families, accompanied by its mutual vexations. Divorces are an expensive pastime.

I know this is ridiculous, but next I felt that if I suddenly renewed contact you would interpret it as my wanting to share in your success in radio and television, to which I had contributed zilch.

I eventually became a bit more mature. I had married again and we raised two daughters, happily. I decided to do my damnedest to become some sort of belated father to you, the toddler I left when I was twenty-nine. You were suspicious and angry about my decades of absence. I did my best to talk honestly and diplomatically, and not to get discouraged by setbacks. Grandchildren gave me the chance to play a fun role as grandpa, minus baggage. Over the past decade we've finally got to know a bit about each other. I find it hard to express my emotions but I love our odd new relationship.

To other absentee fathers: Stay in touch, come what may. Keep showing your face. If you're in another city, it's harder to keep up the contact. Man up and do your best anyway. Don't be a quitter, like I was.

OUR MAN OF NOTE

Jack Harrison was eating oysters in the sunshine four days before he died. New to hospital life, he tipped his hat at the palliative-care nurses and asked if he might enjoy the gift of a dozen molluscs in the garden. He wasn't the Messiah, but he did reduce his last supper to a rubble of briny shells on Easter Thursday afternoon.

All week, the corridor outside room 29 was thick with his visitors. They took turns finding a space around his bed and huddled in twos and threes in the corridor. In the waiting room, more friends and family gathered – bewildered at the news Jack's demise was imminent. At eighty-one, the indomitable head of one of Australia's musical families was mortal after all.

His two sons and daughter took turns at the bedside vigil. Accomplished musicians themselves, they propped against a chair a giant poster of the West Australian Symphony Orchestra, their father's other family for a record-breaking forty-two years.

Only five weeks ago, Jack Harrison and my mother were babysitting our three children. We two parents arrived home from dinner to find Jack and Mum bookended on the sofa, breathing quietly in time. Jack's sparse canopy of hair had gone wild, ruffled by sleep. My mother's hair was a halo of white against the grey suede cushion. I made a secret wish for my husband and I to be such a picture of contentment at seventy-six and eighty-one.

Only months earlier, Jack was perched on another sofa, this one at Mum's house. Blowing and drawing on his harmonica, he crooned 'Moon River' to my small daughter. We had our own private concert as the orchestral accompaniment swelled from the speakers behind him. Our two-year-old, sitting beside her 'Jackpa', was mesmerised. Jack's sweet vibrato floated over us as I filmed the two of them on my phone – performer and pint-sized devotee – eight decades apart. Was that Jack's swan-song? '...*dream-maker, you heart-breaker, wherever you're going I'm going your way.*'

Our Huckleberry Jack was one of the family; by Mum's side at every gathering and party. I would detect him fumbling in his pocket as the cake arrived. With ever-perfect timing, he and his mouth organ would strike up a jaunty 'Happy birthday to you', urging on toddlers' efforts to blow out the candles. How will we now have happy birthdays without him?

He was musical royalty in Perth. Even in 1941, when the country was fixated on the grim news overseas, Jack Harrison's talent drew families around their Astors at 8 pm on a Thursday. That program was *Australia's Amateur Hour.* Jack was hailed a boy wonder, aged ten, taking out the national competition with his mouth-organ.

At twelve, his dad Bill suggested the clarinet. Jack, with his twin sister and elder brother became Jack Harrison's Dance Band. After national radio exposure, pop-star status was theirs at dance halls everywhere. By the time the twins were fifteen, the quartet was earning so much money Jack's dad pulled him out of Scotch College. He'd been a ratbag there anyway: 'They called me king of the cuts', he recalled with pride.

At nineteen, Jack joined the WA Symphony Orchestra. Later, as principal clarinettist, his great set of pipes and rakish wit earned him notoriety and admiration. Never one to create a scene, he nonetheless had a gift for 'a few short yet piquant words delivered with perfect timing at exactly the right volume'. The visiting Austrian conductor Henry Krips once asked him: 'Please, I want it again, Mr Harrison, I want a more peasant tone.'

Jack: 'Sorry to disappoint – I think I left my peasant mouth at home.'

He was well-known for waving a post-modernist score over his head and demanding the 'asbestos test' when the jarring music made him grit his teeth.

Baffled conductor: 'The asbestos test?'

'Yes, let's set it on fire and see if it burns.'

Jack was a sucker for his mum Edna's speciality: crumbed brains in parsley sauce…In 1973, he donned a hard hat, lifted his clarinet and honked out the first note heard in the newly completed Perth Concert Hall…And his death reduced to tears the postie, Rob, who'd been stocking his letterbox in Claremont for five years.

Like so many others, in the days before he died I sat briefly by his gurney and held his hand. I left behind a hand-drawn card from my middle son: 'To Ackpa, get well soon' – with three newly-mastered love-hearts. Jack's body betrayed only subtle signs of his consuming illness: the constant tiredness, a cough, a temperature. For us, there was barely time for the shock to settle. How will we resume our lives now he is gone?

During one of his last lucid moments I whispered: 'What will Mum do without you?' He squeezed my hand and with his eyes still closed, he replied: 'I'm afraid I will have to do without her.'

Jack Harrison: 1931–2013.

THE STORY OF LIFE

It was his email that intrigued me:

> 'You have no clue what really happens when you get old. My wife of 55 years has been taken from me by illness. Maybe one day you could visit her in the nursing home. She is in room 19. Her name is Ada.'
> Warm regards, Carl, 87.

The following day, on a whim, I drive out to the aged-care home. It's a secure facility. A cleaner notices me waiting expectantly on the visitor's side of the door. She punches in the security code, then pads noiselessly away on her soft soles, leaving me to guess which of the deserted corridors to search first. I inhale that haunting scent – the staleness of life at its lowest ebb. It's the same miasma I recall from the nursing home where my nan died – the smell of confinement, unease and antiseptic.

I knock gently on the door of Room 19 and hear a chair scrape as someone gets up to open the door. 'I told her you'd come!' Carl beams at me. 'Come and meet my beauty.'

He still has his veteran's pride: khaki trousers with a sharp crease up the thigh, a pressed short-sleeved shirt, shiny chestnut brogues. Only his hearing aid and the Velcro bandage gripping his wrist hint at any outward signs of decline.

His wife, Ada, is slumped awkwardly in the bed, a slip of a woman in a voluminous cream nightie dotted with cornflowers. Her spindly arms and papery skin stand out in relief against the fat, dimpled pillows stacked behind her. She's breathing noisily, her lids drooped over cloudy eyes. Carl smooths a wayward wisp of her fairy-floss hair.

'She's not coming back to me is she?' We both know the answer. 'Two of her brothers had Parkinsons' he continues, 'and now she's started with the tremors. I give her a kiss and she gives me ten in return!' We both smile.

A nurse rattles in with lunch and briskly suggests we wait outside. 'Ada's refusing to eat', Carl explains, and leads me to two plastic chairs in the corridor.

He is surprisingly buoyant. 'This is my world now. Sitting with her hour after hour, then going home to a cold bed. I want you to write what it's like to grow old: always looking back at life over your shoulder.'

He points to an elderly gent leaning precariously forward in his wheelchair. 'That's Ray', Carl says. The wheelchair's foot rests are folded up and out of the way and Ray is using his slippered feet to inch along the carpet. 'The week after he moved here to be with his wife, she passed away. He doesn't realise she's gone. He spends his whole day shuffling from room to room looking for her.' Ray looks searchingly at me as he edges his wheelchair past us: 'Do you know where they've taken her?' I am moved to tears.

Carl stares at the burgundy leaf-pattern in the carpet while I collect myself. 'I met Ada on the bus, you know', he says. 'I came to Fremantle after the war. I was a frontline interpreter. I'm Dutch, but I speak four languages so the Yanks wanted me.'

He opens his wallet and pulls out a small plastic sleeve. He tips a pebble into my hand. 'Grenade' he tells me. 'They took this shrapnel out of me leg. I howled like a baby. Ada always told me I was a big sook.'

'She tricked me into marrying her, you know', he says. 'I'm Catholic. My family back home didn't want no Church of England girl. She says to me one day: Can you take me to Hehir Street?'

'I know that street' I says to her. 'Little church there.'

'We arrive at the church and the priest says to me: Know what you're here for?'

'Ada had gone and got herself converted. We got married three weeks later.' He leans into me and says: 'You girls got your ways of getting your man!'

We're allowed back into Ada's room. 'She still won't eat' the nurse tells Carl, as she pushes the lunch trolley out the door. He lifts Ada's limp arm and nestles it in his. The veins at her wrist are ropey and tinged with green. The lingering remains of a soft-pink manicure stain her nails.

Carl reaches over to the bedside table and picks up a hand mirror with a long gilt handle. He holds it so Ada can see her reflection: 'Look at those rosy cheeks!' he coos, but Ada doesn't register.

'I just want my wife back,' he says. I see a tear slide down his cheek.

He leans in and plants a kiss on Ada's slackened mouth. We sit in silence by her bedside. Ada shifts in the bed, swallows uncomfortably. Her eyes focus, settling on her husband. Her voice is trembly with the effort of speech but there's no mistaking what she whispers: 'I see a beautiful face.' And then she turns her head away and stares unblinkingly at the door.

Ada Caubo – 24/3/1928 – 13/11/2013.

MENAGERIES

PIGGERY-POKERY, PORKERS CAN FLY

Gertie is my new creature of fascination at the family farm. I've never stood nose-to-snout with a 200-kilo pregnant pig before. Even her head is twice the size of mine. I couldn't work out how her enormous girth didn't topple those four spindly trotters.

I noticed how her giant belly jiggled and rippled as she scratched her bristly thigh against the metal grille of the trailer. I knew then we'd be friends because she made me feel petite. Really, the only attractive thing about her was the patterns in the veins of her ears, backlit in the afternoon sun. But I felt strangely maternal towards her – she was huffing and snorting, much like I did when heavily pregnant. I couldn't believe this gargantuan lump of pork was herself only nine months old.

Gertie had been bought from an out-of-town piggery and the hour-long ride in the back of a trailer was clearly not her idea of fun. Her loud grunts rang out over the front paddock as she arrived, causing much muddlement amongst the three free-range pigs who already call the farm home.

Bruce, Doris and Evelyn, at six months old, are swine teenagers – featherweights at 150 kilos apiece. Doris and Evelyn are best friends and adore their boar, Bruce. I can see why, as he sports a pair of testicles the size of rockmelons. But here was a new piece of tail to tempt Bruce. As the first whiff of the aromatic Gertie sailed downwind across the pig paddock, Bruce began pacing the fence, frothing at the snout.

My brother-in-law reversed the ute up to the yard and wrenched open the trailer gate. Gertie stumbled down the ramp. Bruce, squealing and grunting through his foaming beard, jammed his snout firmly in Gertie's rump. Doris, in a jealous rage, rounded on Gertie, trying to sink her teeth into her rival's hind leg.

Gertie took off round the yard trying to escape the fury of two envious sows and the lecherous boar. Sensing we might be in for some R-rated violence and/or sex scenes, I herded my six-year-old son and his little sister into the ute: 'Quick!' I yelled, 'Hop in where it's safe.' The cacophony of pig squeals almost drowned out the chorus of complaints from the back seat: 'Mum! Mum! We can't see!'

Gertie then made a snap decision.

She gave herself a good run-up and barged across the yard as fast as those gristly trotters would allow. The next thing I knew, she was hurling herself over the steel fence like Steve McQueen in *The Great Escape*. Front legs clear, her low-slung belly caught the top rail. I winced, thinking of the embedded piglets, but she had just enough momentum to drag her hind legs up and over. Gertie landed clumsily on the freedom side of the fence. From inside their paddock, Bruce, Doris and Evelyn were struck mute as Gertie cantered off down the hill towards the dam.

Heading back to Perth that night, and with Gertie still on the run, we pleaded for regular updates on the escapee. Pigs are nothing new for my brother-in-law, who manages the farm. His father was once a butcher in Collie, renowned for his 'Ding' sausages. The recipe was secret but those bangers earned folklore status in a town where snags are one of the five food groups.

Five days later the phone rang: 'Gertie's back! I went up to feed Bruce and the girls and there she was, snuffling around the yard like nothing happened!'

I suggested Gertie was suffering from Stockholm syndrome, and had decided she was better off befriending the swines who tried to attack her than going it alone in the bush.

A month later, and Gertie has farrowed. She is mother to three little pigs.

The kids and I save our vegetable peelings and burnt toast for her. We wade through the long grass in the old orchard, collecting the apples felled by birds or chewed by possums. As Gertie hears the quad bike approach, she charges out of her half tank, upending her sleeping piglets.

I am revolted by her table manners, which remind me of dinners at home. Pig gluttony is grotesque but mesmerising. Gertie suctions up half a bucket of pellets and a large bowl of scraps, then she's shoving her piglets out the way to see if I brought dessert.

The farm is harmonious once again: Bruce has gone off the boil now the piglets are permanently attached to Gertie's pink bosoms. Doris and Evelyn are no longer green-eyed. We're all basking in the glow of porcine motherhood. The kids and I hang around the pig pen watching Gertie tolerate the antics of her piglets. Her parental indifference is contagious: I barely react when my three-year-old feeds Gertie a large slice of quiche Lorraine.

I hope the children remember Gertie's great escape. Few kids are lucky enough to witness 200 kilos of pork sailing over a metre-high fence. Who says pigs can't fly!

LISTENING DEVICES

Between man and wife, listening is an art form. It is an elusive skill, requiring mental endurance and an air-traffic controller's concentration. (In our house, most conversations are near misses between my mouth and his ears.) Moreover, listening requires self control – the word *listen* contains the same letters as the word *silent*. My family has no restraint. Usually, we're too busy interrupting one another to hear what's being said.

The man of the house, however, has turned marital listening into an exercise in subterfuge. He has enough rat-cunning to convince me he's paying attention to my every word, while really, he's keeping track of the cricket score over my shoulder.

At stumps, I poked my head into his office and said: 'By the way honey, what did you decide about tomorrow night?' He flashed me a meretricious smile: 'Whatever you like, Blossom. I'm easy. You're the social secretary, remember?'

And then our conversation degenerated into this tiresome patter:

'(Sigh) You don't know what I'm talking about, do you?'

'Depends...'

'Depends on what? Geez! Do you ever listen to a word I say?!'

'I *was* listening, I just didn't think it was important enough to remember.'

Listening is now a prickly aspect of our relationship. I admit I do most of the talking, but he does most of the ignoring. To help himself annoy me more, my husband has mastered a second language: a vocabulary of eye rolls, gruntlets, exasperated head shaking and a raised right eyebrow (of doom). He uses these to stymie all conversation so he can continue reading about Nigella Lawson's cocaine habit in peace.

I get bored unless I'm talking. I like to fill the gaps between conversations with commentary. During the Sunday night movie I get in trouble for asking perfectly legitimate questions:

'Hey! Is that Terence Stamp? Man! He's aged hasn't he? No, no, it's Alan Rickman, isn't it? Yup, it's Alan Rickman. He was so good as the bad guy in *Die Hard*, remember honey? He had that amazing German accent.'

And then my bloke rocks his head on his neck and his right eyebrow strains to push up a forehead wrinkle:

'No, it's not Terence Stamp and it's not Alan Rickman, it's Charles Dance. Now will you please be quiet. I've proven to you I'm listening, all right?'

And then I squeeze his hand and snuggle into his hairy left thigh because I know Alan Rickman when I see him.

Of course, we now have another listening problem creeping into our relationship. Apparently I don't just have a talking problem, I have a hearing problem. No matter that my bloke has a mumbling problem.

He likes to mumble with his back to me. He talks to me sotto voce from his office down the hall. He thinks his conversation is so riveting I should be craning my neck to hear what he has to say. I've now been forced into a speech pattern that begins with 'Pardon?' And he's cheesed off with having to repeat himself.

I wonder if my years in radio damaged my ears? I always wore the cans lopsided, covering my right ear, exposing my left, so I didn't have to hear myself booming in stereo – mono was disconcerting enough. Maybe my right ear got sick of listening to my voice? Maybe my left ear went out in sympathy?

My teenage son likes to mock my hearing by playing me high-frequency tones on his iPod. While everyone in the house is screwing up their faces and sticking their fingers in their ears, I blithely continue stacking the dishwasher. (Raising three children gives me enormous tolerance for high-pitched shrieks and wails.)

And then thirteen-year-old son guffaws: 'Hey Mum! Can't you hear that? Are you deaf? It's hurting my ears!'

So now I'm being dared to have a hearing test because my husband mumbles and my son plays stupid test-tones only dogs and flappy-eared children can hear.

I have no trouble hearing the sixty-decibel repartee of my two best girlfriends. We oracles know each other so intimately we don't even call it listening: we call it waiting our turn to talk. But I was nonplussed the other day, at our favourite cafe, when one of my besties leaned into me and said: 'Luvvy, I think you may be shouting.'

'I'm not shouting, I'm just excited about getting a hearing aid.'

Should the espresso machine compete with some really important news, I make sure my smiling and nodding more than compensate for any lack of listening.

So in the interests of marital harmony, I have bowed to familial pressure and agreed to get a hearing test. I'm not too worried — I had one five years ago and got a near-perfect score. 'Selective deafness', the audiologist whispered to his assistant. He thought I didn't hear him, but I'm brilliant at lip-reading.

MAN ENOUGH

'The bloke' is back. I know this because I went to the Medieval Fair in York. Never have I seen so many grunting he-men in one sweltering paddock.

I was at a loose end a few Sundays back. My two smallest urchins needed an adventure while their father was away. As I pulled off the highway into York at 10 am, the gauge in my car read thirty-four degrees. I cruised along Balladong street looking for a shady park. Six-year-old son spotted a hulk of a man crossing the street in chest plate and chain mail. 'Look Mum! It's a dress-up! He's wearing a metal skirt!'

'Yes, honey. We've entered the Dark Ages. That chain mail frock is called a hauberk. It stops a sword from cutting your legs.' His eyes were saucers, so I notched up a gear.

'See his big sword? It's so sharp he could cut slice you in half with one blow!'

Three-year-old daughter wailed: 'I wanna go home!'

Her brother, shocked at the grim and gritty business of trial by combat, grabbed her hand: 'Don't worry. We'll still get an ice-cream.'

We three peasants joined the queue of gentlefolk squashing through the makeshift gate. We shuffled forward and handed the festival wench a tenner.

Inside the fairground, bosomy CWA matrons were peddling Christmas cakes and heraldic tea towels. Big fellas in velvet tunics and hessian trousers were flogging home-made weapons. 'What's this called?' asked my youngster, pointing at a knife with a slender blade.

'That, my young man, is a stiletto.'

I smirked. 'Yep, my feet kill in those!'

The weapons merchant leaned in towards my boy: 'Your ma's a smarty-pants i'nt she?!' My six-year-old agreed, then spotted a chain-mail tunic hanging from the awning: 'What's that?'

'Aah, that one's got a strange name too – it's called a cuirass. Can you say that? *Cweer-aaas.*'

'Plenty of them 'round here!' (I was on a roll.)

He cocked a shaggy eyebrow at me.

'Let's go get an ice-cream!' I said, wishing medieval shopkeepers didn't take themselves so seriously. We trooped off to the *Penny Farthing Sweets* van.

An ear-splitting metallic screech shook the crowd. Small daughter clapped her hands over her ears. Then a baritone boomed over the loudspeaker: 'Hear ye! Hear ye! Geoffrey the Blaggard of York will duel to the death with the imposter El Sid from Goomalling. Mark my words, blood will be spilled today.'

At that moment, I heard a *chink-chink-chink* and turned to see an armoured giant half as wide as he was tall heading towards us. Small daughter darted behind my legs.

He wore a black helmet that jutted over his forehead, leaving two metal slits for his eyes. A wild gingery beard joined up with the shag pile on his chest. His XXXX girth strained against a belt that held a five-pronged mace in its scabbard. The crowd peeled back to let him pass.

His opponent, El Sid from Goomalling, was a dark knight with curls and brooding looks. 'Today is a fine day to die!' he bellowed, and we reciprocated with cheering, clapping and snickering.

And so the bludgeon fight began. The mob roared its appreciation for two beefcakes sweating it out in full armour on a baking hot day. While my children gaped from behind the rope fence, I cast my gaze at the throng.

There were no vapid metrosexuals on display here. I was a maiden amongst the countryside's best brawn: men in mud-caked boots, faded Levis and wraparound sunnies. There wasn't a pastel polo-shirt or a pair of suede loafers in sight. For the first time since my high school ball, I felt petite.

I turned back to the arena to see El Sid using his murderous blows to annihilate the home town hero. Geoffrey the Blaggard, his throat slit, collapsed in mock agony, writhing in the hot sand and grass clippings. The kids were speechless.

We wandered back to the car as Geoffrey revived himself with a stubbie of VB. I reflected that even the out-of-town blokes looked manful today with their burly chests and thickets of leg hair.

Making a rare trip to St Georges Terrace last Friday, I was perplexed by the male vanity on parade. By lunchtime, the city was teeming with dandies flaunting their over-pumped torsos, finicky hairstyles and stage-managed stubble. Is this what women want?

The man's man I live with has no truck with titivation. He's a retrosexual – the kind who hails the Dunlop Volley as the greatest sandshoe ever made. A guy who carries his six-pack in a brown paper bag. I tolerate his quirks because I don't want a bloke who primps more than I do.

Later, on the drive back to Perth, I asked my youngster which part of the Medieval Fair he'd liked the most. Was it the bruising contests in the arena? The gruesome armaments? The Herculean warriors?

'I liked the honey-tasting best', he said. But the raspberry ice-cream came a close second.

IN A CAT FLAP

I've always been a cat person. I don't like to admit it because cat people are snooty and aloof and picky about their food. Dog people, on the other hand, are irrepressibly gleeful and outdoorsy and are always excited to see you.

I have tried to become a dog person, because dog people are universally liked. They don't know meanness or envy or discontent. But it's their dogs I don't like: dogs who press their wet noses, like cold liver, into my crotch. Dogs with big teeth and drippy tongues who clumsily paw at me in greeting (and not in the nice way my husband does it). Or dogs with stumpy legs who've tuned their bark into a shrill yap-yap-yap that makes me wince. I see dog people in clumps at the park in the evenings and feel jealous. I catch a drift of their doggy conversations as I dig holes in the sandpit and fetch balls for my children: 'What a lovely shiny coat! What do you feed her?' I hear one fellow say to a cocker-spaniel owner. (I try to avoid shiny coats – they add three kilos.) 'What breed is he?' asks another. I want to yell out: 'I'd like to see your pedigree, you mongrel!' but I have too much breeding.

Dog people live their lives on display. They're always promenading around our park looking relaxed and contented as this frazzled mother herds her children across the oval to the school gate. On the way home, I feel obliged to stop and coo over the neighbourhood's Tibetan spaniel the way I gush over babies in prams.

I like to laugh at dogs hanging out of car windows as much as the next person. I just don't want to drive with one barking at nothing in my ear as I try to change lanes on the freeway. For me, getting a dog would be like taking on another child, and I'm still trying to train the three I've got. A cat is all I have time for. Cat owners don't meet in the park every evening. They have no such camaraderie. They think being labelled a social recluse is a compliment.

So the kids and I troop off to the Cat's Refuge Home – half a dozen sheds full of deserted moggies. It's quiet and clean and all the pussycats are curled up in their cages napping, or being aloof and arrogant – knowing they're too beautiful to be homeless for long. I ask the sourpuss attendant if the kids and I can go in and pat them: 'You'll need to gown up first.' Like incompetent surgeons wrapped in our crunchy plastic aprons, we try to sterilise our hands with pink pump-action goop. The kids are competing to make the most noise by crackling their gowns. The attendant frowns at us, then stalks out of the shed. We four are left alone with a clowder of cats.

And then we spot Alfie. He is the smallest and pounciest of a litter of abandoned kittens, a piebald mop of fluff. Above his little white mouth is a two-finger black moustache just like Hitler's.

I immediately feel sorry for him – how could the kitty gene pool be so unkind? I pick him up and give him a cuddle. I tell him that it was Charlie Chaplin who first sported the toothbrush moustache in 1914, well before Hitler. Alfie breaks into a tiny purr.

Then smallest child trips over her scrubs, and Alfie – startled – wriggles free from my arms and performs a forward somersault in the pike position before landing lightly on the ground. We all agree he's talented enough to come home with us.

At the counter, I buy a $150 kitten, $64 worth of kitty litter and $40 worth of vet-recommended biscuits. Sourpuss attendant, all smiles now, says Alfie will also need an identity chip fitted under his skin in case he gets lost. I book him in for next week: 'If I bring my three-year-old along, can you fit one in her as well?'

Now we are a family of five plus a cat. Alfie is loved by everyone in the house, which is just as well, because within a week I've had it up to pussy's bow with his kitty litter scattered like gravel all over the laundry floor.

And the pet shop – who knew? There are two-storey cat-houses with carpet on the mezzanine. There is a $140, four-post cat scratcher made of seagrass. And there are cat jumpers (small and medium – tough luck if you're a fat cat). Collars can have diamonds or sequins, or scary-looking studs (for bikies' cats).

I went there to find a cheap cane basket for Alfie to sleep in, but all the cat beds on display had Posturepedic mattresses and (fake) fur doonas. With no cane baskets in sight, I choose the cheapest bed in the shop: black igloo-style with white paws stamped all over it. I was embarrassed walking back to the car with my $50 pet igloo but a couple I passed gave me a wink and a smile. They must have been dog owners.

ANYONE LOST A SET OF DENTURES?

The scariest teeth I've known belonged to a Grade 7 teacher called Mr Campbell. They dominated his face in the same way as Mister Ed's – horsey and over-sized. In fearsome combination with his gravelly baritone (which exploded like a sonic boom when angry), choirmaster Campbell and his big choppers are all I remember about singing lessons.

To my four-foot nothing, his six-foot something appeared gargantuan. He strode around the music room on his leg-stilts with his head cocked to one side, straining to identify which one of us was out of tune. My thin soprano would peter out to a squeak as soon as Mr Campbell leaned over and put his ear to my mouth. Unimpressed, he would restore himself to his full height and grimace before moving on to find the owner of the flat notes.

Memories of his gritted teeth came flooding back last week as the kids and I were shedding our beach sand under the open-air shower at North Cott.

There they sat: the top row of a set of dentures, sunning themselves on the retaining wall. My two-year-old daughter pounced on them thinking they were an exotic shell to put in her bucket. Five-year-old son was more cautious: 'Mum, did that thing really come from the sea?' Twelve-year-old son's disgust turned to horror when his sister shouted: 'Can the teef come home with us?' and jammed those dentures sideways into her mouth, using both her hands to try to make them fit.

'Spit them out!' I yelled.

She did, and they landed upside down in the shower, the plastic palate filling up with a little puddle.

I gingerly collected those disembodied cuspids, washed them off and set them back in their sunny spot on the retaining wall to await their owner. But after ten minutes, it was clear no-one was missing their front teeth enough to consider them lost.

That encounter with the contents of someone else's mouth got me thinking about my husband's grandfather (unforgettably named Fred Smith). He was the dentist in Collie for forty years. His pet hate was going to parties and having guests whip out their wet dentures to show him where they were chafing. He got his own back pinning patients to the dentist's chair with his famously giant belly and they got to hear the gurgling of what he'd had for lunch.

Fred Smith flung all the rotten teeth he extracted out the back door of his surgery into his veggie patch. Aunty Lin, Fred's youngest daughter, delighted in digging them up and playing knucklebones with her gruesome treasures.

It's rare to see shocking teeth these days. Modern dentistry has given us whiteners and veneers, braces, crowns and caps – all kinds of costumes to disguise the ugliness within our mouths. But historians are fascinated with bad teeth. Josephine Bonaparte's smile was said to resemble a 'mouthful of cloves'. One scholar reported her teeth 'looked like an oyster lease at low tide'.

Queen Elizabeth I was renowned for her blackened teeth – being addicted to sweets and fearful of the primitive dentistry of the day. For centuries, portraits of the nobility only showed a tight smile: it was left to the lower classes to display their poor breeding with a cheerfully jagged grin. By the 1800s, the Georgians had realised a 'fine set of snappers' was needed for genteel-sounding speech and to show off the 'ornaments of the mouth.' A well-kept toothy smile was obvious proof of prosperity.

In our house, five-year-old son is currently milking the gap in his pegs for all it's worth. A few weekends back on a blustery day, his boogie board flipped up and smacked him in the mouth, dislodging his prized front tooth in a pool of blood on the sand. The tooth fairy left a comforting, over-generous fiver and a note: 'You got off lightly little man, your dad had his front teeth knocked out at uni when a young Troy Buswell unintentionally slammed a door in his face.'

My mother was a stickler for my six-monthly dental visits when I was a child. Our dentist, Mr Hodby, had scary implements but gentle hands. I spent hours of my childhood staring at his ceiling, my body rigid with fear, hands clenched in my lap. I can still picture the swirly patterns of the fibrous cement panels overhead. Like a proper lady on honeymoon, that ceiling is all I remember.

Thanks to Mum, my teeth are still my best feature. In my late twenties, as I was set free from Mr Hodby's chair one day and was walking back to my car, my old music teacher Mr Campbell came striding towards me. He'd shrunk – his legs were no longer stilts. As we passed each other, I wondered 'What about those scarily big teeth?'. So I flashed him a confident smile in the hope he'd remember me from choir 1979, front row, squeaky soprano. He smiled back at me, politely, not a hint of recognition, revealing a row of neat white teeth, no bigger than mine. Quite a nice smile, actually. And away he went.

CONSUMING PASSIONS

'What if I look like mutton dressed as sheep?' I ask the lissom sales girl. It's a legitimate question: I'm trying on a frock in attention-seeking scarlet. Actually, it's more a shade of watermelon. I'm worried I'll look like one in it.

She looks at me blankly and continues preening herself in the mirror next to mine. She's been stalking round the shop on her leg-stilts like some exotic wading bird, a riot of colour in flowing jungle-print. I crane my neck because she is wearing this summer's four-inch platforms and I'm straight from the beach in my purple thongs, circa 2010.

'Go on', she coaxes. 'Spoil yourself – it's Christmas!'

And there it is: an invitation to conspicuous consumption. Her words stick to my brain like cheap tinsel puttied to shop windows. I agree with her anyway: 'I'll take it!'

'It fits you like a glove,' she calls over her shoulder as she heads briskly over to the till. I give myself a last once-over in the mirror, unsure whether to believe her. The dress does fit rather snugly (perhaps not so much glove as fireman's gauntlet). I hand her my Mastercard and she plucks it daintily from me with a well-practiced flourish.

Clutching my gilt-edged carry-bag, $249 poorer, I exit the shop giddy with my impulse buy. I am high on shopper's euphoria.

By the time I've rounded up a BBQ chicken and a twelve-pack of toilet rolls at Coles, I have dress-buyer's remorse. I already own frocks I love more than this clingy one. I always feel garish in red. Why blow $250 on something I'm too timid to wear?

Trudging home, I observe my fellow shoppers too, are weighed down by their new purchases. Up ahead, I notice a handsome woman with a platinum helmet of hair bearing down on me. Her arms are strung with dress-shop bags, their (glamorously) sharp corners bouncing against her legs as she sashays through the arcade.

Can we pass without colliding? Her gaze is somewhere above my head, so making eye contact with this superior being is out of the question. Sensing an imminent sideswipe, I step to my left. She marches past me unimpeded (and ungrateful). It is a vulgar display.

I wonder if my haughty friend is annoyed I didn't step out of her way sooner. Perhaps she wanted my envy for her shopping spree. All I sensed was an aggressive attempt at one-upmanship.

By the time I get home, I have concocted a rationale for my own splurge. My red dress reclines artfully on the bed while I rummage through my wardrobe for shoes to match.

For a few moments, I am again drunk with pleasure, but then my satisfaction turns to something ugly: a slavish craving for more. I want the tan-coloured wedges I spotted last week. Should I splash out and buy the filigree necklace I've been lusting after all year? I've waited long enough, haven't I?

Part of me hankers for reckless extravagance. Or perhaps it's schadenfreude – that same perverse satisfaction I get from reading *New Weekly* in the hairdresser and seeing Miley Cyrus being shunned for trying too hard to be controversial.

Had I had access to money as a teenager, I too would have succumbed to shopping gluttony and bought myself a pair of Reebok hi-top sneakers and a perm. Instead, I spent my $12 pocket money on McCalls' dress-making patterns. I spread those brown paper cut-outs all over the loungeroom floor. Then I tacked together my version of the flouncy denim skirt Brooke Shields wore while shipwrecked in *The Blue Lagoon*. Sewing those crooked seams on Mum's old Husqvarna took the best part of a Saturday. But I can still recall the kick I got out of looking bespoke the entire summer of 1980.

Strangely, I cannot remember a single Christmas present I received as a kid. And yet I envied my well-off friends their new Starfire white rollerskates and Nintendo Game Boys. My temptation now is to spoil my offspring. Last week I asked my teenager his favourite thing about Christmas. I expected 'presents' to top his list. 'The Santa Claus footprints you used to dust around the fireplace with icing sugar' came the reply. (He'd got wise one year and licked the floor.)

I still get a childish thrill from hauling our dusty box of Christmas decorations up from the garage. I lift lopsided stars and strange glittery creatures from their tissue-paper nests and tell my kids how old they were when they made them. They beg me to make shortbread so they can use the reindeer cookie-cutters and sneak glacé cherries from the bowl. We go for night drives with all the windows down counting how many houses are strung with fairy lights. It's the leadup to Christmas I love – the day itself is always an anti-climax.

Oh, and whatever happened to my new red dress? Actually I bought it last Christmas. I still haven't plucked up the courage to become a scarlet woman.

OBJECTS OF AFFECTION

GETTING IN A BIND OVER A FIX

I am not the person you call on to get something fixed. Unless it's a missing button, a sandwich or a broken heart. Year 8 home economics and the empathy gene have served me well, but not well enough to be trusted with important things like dishwashers that don't, taps that drip like nightly water torture, and new digital tellies that refuse to play ball when the tennis starts.

Every household needs someone who has patience, logic and the ability to read an instruction manual. Apparently I have none of these skills. Actually, I know I have none of these skills because I switch off the minute the man of the house starts lecturing me about why domestic life might be easier if I kept my cool, attempted some rational thought and located the darn instruction manual.

I've already learnt one of the most important lessons for marital harmony: decide which one of you is going to play the helpless role, and which of you is going to pretend they know what they're doing. I don't like to tread on my husband's area of expertise – self delusion – because he prides himself on his masterful tool-work.

Our garage, depending on your point of view, is either an obsessive-compulsive's shrine to hoarding or a spider-pit of uselessness. Countless bits of sawn-off skirting boards have been stacked on the rafters, all manner of timber offcuts festoon the walls, some rusted gardening tools first used to topiary the gardens of Versailles are propped behind the door and there's a kayak whose bottom has been wet just the once (by the sprinkler). Trying to coax a hoarder into sending scraps of wood to the tip is like asking a kid to give up Christmas. I get a staunch refusal backed up by some pithy remark: 'If I ever got some time to myself on a weekend I'd be oar-in-hand down the river right now!' Little does he know that over the years, I've portered trunkfuls of his prized junk across town to friends' verges, awaiting their council 'bring out your dead'.

When my jack-of-all-trades is fed up with his squabbling progeny interrupting the cricket on weekends, he grabs his car keys and calls to me over his shoulder: 'I'm just popping down to Bunnings, do you need anything?' I like to yell back: 'I'd like a new set of knockers please, wooden ones if they have them, they feel nice. Oh, and an all-purpose spreader.' In case he doesn't know what I'm talking about, I add: 'And some lawn fertilizer to put in it.' Then I sit back and make a cup of tea knowing he'll be gone for hours because Bunnings is his Aladdin's cave.

I'm sure the place is also a cult. Customers in Bunnings look disconcertingly happy – like they're high on the sheer spectacle of a million bits and bobs within easy reach (of a fork-lift). I notice there's a lot of waiting around at the paint counter, but everybody is calm – people making small talk with each other while they finger the silky new paintbrushes. I see their eyes glaze over as they fantasise about new colour swatches and virgin rollers and trays, all fluffy-soft and inviting. No-one does their lolly there, even when it takes fifteen minutes to locate the plumbing expert and the queue at the cash register is a dozen deep.

Objects of Affection

My right-hand man uses trips to Bunnings as a rite of passage for our five-year-old. Together, man and boy drive off in the ute and vanish for half the afternoon, signalling their return with a flurry of excited shouts: 'Hey, I got a really big tool box, some new drill bits, a hot dog and a piece of special wood.' And then I turn to my small son and say 'And what did you get darling?'

I know there might be just as many women as men who love fixing things. But I doubt it. Though I do have several girlfriends who have been forced into the role of household trouble-shooter by necessity. Like me, there are men out there who won't read instruction manuals – believe it or not. They're usually the ones who have 'tool tempers' that erupt while hanging (their wives') paintings – where the air turns blue from their constant stream of invective and the hallway is littered with hooks and screws thrown down from the ladder in disgust. Those kinds of tinkerers need to accept their limitations, hand the drill and plugs to the missus and dish out instructions instead.

To me, a washing machine is as complex as a space shuttle, so when I'm left alone in a house with a malfunctioning appliance, I feel uncomfortable. Last month our toilet threatened to block because our two-year-old thinks 'toilet training' is teaching the bog to swallow an entire roll of poo-tickets. Having fished reams of sodden paper out of the bowl, my bloke fiddled around with the flush mechanism and pronounced it 'fixed'.

As he left the house for work the next morning, I was given strict instructions to gently press the button until the water subsided. Gentle pressing I did, but when the water started rising – fast – I did what any level-headed woman would do and started frantically bashing the button. It worked a treat. Until the button stopped being a button and got stuck in the hole. I thought I might sort it out if I lifted the cistern lid off and had a play around, but some valve popped out of alignment and then I couldn't get the lid back on. Knowing I was faced with certain disgrace, I rang three plumbers before one agreed to call by, fixed it in thirty seconds and charged me $90 for the pleasure. Frankly, it was a small price to pay for saving my bacon.

Domestic life is not just divided into do-it-yourself-ers and incompetents. It's about who kills the cockroaches, especially the summer ones that rocket into the house with their Boeing wingspans. It's about which half of a partnership likes spiders enough to slide them out the back door on a piece of newspaper without histrionics. And it's which person wakes up fast enough to make a flying leap from bed when there are scary noises in the middle of the night. It's never a burglar, always middle son falling out of bed. His father usually gets the trailing foot tangled up in the sheet and traumatises all three children with howls of shock and pain as he crashes to the floor.

Misbehaving computers, however, are a burden to be shared equally. When they go on the blink, or blank, I yell for my forty-six-year-old technology wizard, who tells me (much too gleefully): 'Isn't it time you learnt to fix it yourself?'

'Help!' I then plead to eldest son, who calls back: 'You're such a noob Mum, you can't even find your own Word document – Epic Fail.' I tell him to lower his voice so my cover's not blown – really, I have no idea how to retrieve any documents from the Microsoft cloud, but hey – I don't need that telegraphed.

I don't believe anyone should be facetious about maintenance matters. When the dishwasher improves to washing eighty per cent of the dishes and sodden husband finally emerges from inside it, I hand him a glass of wine to reward his genius and remark: 'Thanks honey, you're quite a catch.' (Dishwashers are not all he can get going.)

Last law of marital harmony: appreciate the effort, not the result. (Then get a professional in first thing Monday.)

RACKING UP THE YEARS

My first bra came from Jayne Mansfield's closet. At least it felt like it did. It was pale pink satin and doubled as a bullet-proof vest. The label said 'Action' bra but that was the last thing I was going to get in it. The hooks at the back were large enough to catch herring, there was not a skerrick of elastic for comfort and I needed to be Houdini to get in or out of it. Houdini, or a locksmith.

That bra came from the bottom of Mum's drawer of antiquity and I'm pretty sure the cups hadn't seen breasts since 1953. But I was thirteen and desperate. It was Thursday night, there was school on Friday and late-night shopping hadn't been invented. My breasts and I could not face another round of heckling from the leering boys who hung on the fence watching our school softball.

That afternoon, my bra-less dash round the bases clinched the game – but my breasts must have sailed over the home plate before I did, because those boys started cheering: 'Hey yer headlights 'r' on! Yer blinding us with yer high beams!'

I was deflated. And humiliated. So that night, Mum dug through her cupboard and unearthed her heirloom bra. I thought I was going to be swallowed in it, but if it kept my particulars under wraps, I was prepared to wear it. And so began a complicated relationship with my breasts.

For thirty years, I have re-played that bra-less home run as my Bo Derek moment. Me: nubile gazelle-woman, running in slow motion, nothing jiggling, just a gentle swaying up front, spectators mesmerised. That was until I took up jogging last year and the man of the house watched me stumble in through the gate: 'Hey blossom, Dudley Moore would have been proud of that running style. Even sober.'

Having worn a bra since 1980, I've grown accustomed to constriction. (Breasts that don't move are my objective now.) But women are never happy with what they've got. Breasts are always too small, too pointy, too cumbersome or just too big: those boobs so outspoken they take all the male attention off your face: 'Hey soldier – eyes up and front!'

Why are men still fixated on breasts when half the population has them? And why are there so many names for them? There are photos of my mum in the fifties in bras so pointy they could take your eye out: 'Look at the lungs on that sheila!' By the sixties bosoms were 'Bristol cities' and winging it freestyle. In the seventies, *A Clockwork Orange* called them 'Groodies' and then foxy mammas went disco: 'Check out the rack on that chick!' In 1982, Jane Fonda dressed her Pointer Sisters in lycra and aerobics took over the gym. By the time I was at school we were comparing 'hooters' and girls with 'bodacious ta-tas' were flaunting their assets every chance they got.

Now I notice two types of women: those who dress for the breast and those who don't – women are either offence or defence. Some breasts are so properly controlled they're stand-offish. Others aren't shy *enough* – they're in your face everywhere – spilling out of the waitress' uniform as she takes your order, or blindsiding you in the supermarket aisle.

I pity men confronted with a pair of barely contained breasts. Cleavage a woman can hide her keys in is like a car crash – no man can look away. I can't either.

Fashionable women disguise their breasts in Wonderbras and push-ups, minimisers, firmers and separators. Breasts can be made to look bigger, higher, friskier. It's not until we get them home that they can really be themselves and relax. (Some relax better than others.)

The breast connoisseur I live with says bosoms quicken his pulse. That's because until he's allowed to unwrap them, he doesn't know what he's going to get: 'I've never been disappointed. I'm just thrilled to see them in the wild at all.'

My breasts have served me well. They've done their hard work putting fat cheeks on three babies, they've not complained about getting up in the middle of the night or the endless dawn starts.

For that, breasts deserve some respect. Good manners dictate men don't ogle women whose breasts are feeding babies. Or breasts that fall out of bathers while their owner gets dumped in the City Beach surf.

Maybe my breasts need to reclaim their charisma. Now I've finished with the business of procreation and my breasts can go back to being just for fun, I have to juggle them into support mechanisms because they're tired and can't stay up late anymore.

Sometimes the sight of an impossibly pert pair of breasts makes me pine for those days when I didn't realise how good mine were. Breasts start out in life as star-gazers and end up as path-finders, but all breasts get their quality time. I'm okay with what I've got. I think we've finally got the hang of each other.

BORN BUT TO DIE

Here's my conspiracy theory: today's gadgets are made to fail. And here's my evidence: both the vacuum cleaner and my mobile phone have carked it just weeks out of warranty.

Last Sunday, the vacuum cleaner, my trusty servant, stopped dead. The two of us were having a lovely time sucking up all the bits of Lego left lying on the lounge room floor. (We often play games, the vacuum cleaner and I, ferreting about under the sofa with the suction at warp speed. We try to guess from the 'rattle – rattle – clunk!' what mystery object has shot up the hose.)

Always noisy and frolicsome, my appliance was suddenly still. All I could hear was a faint ticking. I rolled its body into the recovery position, ripped open the lid and shook the bag resting limply inside. I smacked the machine shut hoping to restore its noisy breath. Nothing. I squinted up the hose to see if its airway was blocked but I had an unterrupted view of the front door. I emptied the dust filter and pumped the on/off switch with a firm-but-steady rhythm but by now its body was cold.

I had just enough time to race to the electrical shop before it closed. I burst through the door, my expensive Italian clutched in my arms, dribbling fine grey dust from its back end. The bloke behind the counter took one look and said: 'We'll have a crack, luv, but now that it's out of warranty, the drop-off fee is $85' and we charge $65 an hour labour which doesn't cover parts so it might be cheaper to buy a new one.'

I got the feeling he knew something I didn't: my two-year-old vacuum cleaner was built *not* to last. It had what *Choice* magazine calls 'planned obsolescence'. I felt like a chump. Here I was thinking my vacuum and I had a future together, and all the while it was secretly planning career suicide. I forgave the betrayal and begged the electrician: 'I need to know what went wrong, if you can't fix it, I want an autopsy.'

The very next day, my mobile phone crashed in sympathy. An inky blank screen stared back at me. Somewhere inside it were the phone numbers of everyone I know. I went to the Apple store, a place so technologically advanced the geeky staff look uber-cool in their coke-bottle glasses and identical blue polo shirts. Customers, depending on their age, look either confused or euphoric at the smorgasbord of technology laid out before them. At the door, the maitre d'Apple fiddled around with my phone for a minute then suggested: 'Time for an upgrade?' I tried to look euphoric but he sensed my confusion.

'Did you back it up Ma'am?' He already knew the answer so I replied guiltily: 'Please tell me you can restore it? My social life lives inside that phone.'

'Well, if it *can* be fixed, it'll take a couple of weeks. But your screen is cracked and iPhone 4s are pretty outdated now...'

'Okay, okay' I interrupt, 'I get your drift.'

Mobile phones aren't meant to be repaired, they're meant to be upgraded. Superseded by something a little thinner or a little longer so that the charger and the three covers you have at home no longer fit.

I can't get used to the idea that TVs and computers and cameras that are working just fine should be replaced simply because a newer version comes along. It makes me feel gluttonous.

My mother had her Hecla toaster for nearly thirty years. It had doors that flipped down and it never complained no matter how thick the toast we stuffed in it. In Mum's day, broken things were fixed by a generation of menders and make-doers with tweezers and soldering irons. My eldest, twelve, is a whizz at building contraptions, but already, he loves to trade up his gear. How many pairs of headphones are enough? Will PlayStation 3 be embarrassing once PlayStation 4 arrives?

There was nothing terribly wrong with my vacuum cleaner, as it happens, it just had a worn belt. The repair cost me $160 but we are reunited. Now I know my two-year-old Italian is past its prime.

My new phone, however, has been greeted with much excitement by the small members of the house. It'd be even more exciting if I knew the phone number of someone to call, but for now, the phone and I are just a lonely little twosome with lots of fancy icons. My iPhone 5 is so advanced it has a genie inside it called 'Siri' who listens, comments and does whatever I say. 'Call Chelsea Pizza', I demand, and she finds the number and dials it. 'Siri, are you my friend?', I ask her, as the kids guffaw.

'I am not just your friend,' she replies in her husky robotic voice, 'I am your new B-F-F'. The kids are now hysterical. I quietly explain to Siri that the vacuum cleaner and I were once 'Best Friends Forever', but we fell out over some Lego.

THE END OF THE LINE

My home telephone is almost obsolete. It hardly rings any more. Sometimes I forget it's even there. It languishes by the window on my desk, a wallflower obscured by the showy blooms of a potted cyclamen.

I know my home phone is lonely because, as I walk past, it emits a weedy 'peep'. I see its will to live ebbing away, unable to compete with the thrilling gadgetry of my shiny iPhone. I feel sorry for my home phone – trapped by its own limitations – good for talking, and not much else.

When I was a child, the telephone ruled from its own settee. Ours was Bakelite and sat like a black brick on a small lacquered table by the front door, attached to a bench seat upholstered in flocked green velvet. This is where we sat to answer the phone. The handset was a dumbbell, only heavier. Holding it to my ear for more than three minutes made my neck ache. Next to the phone lay a glossy white teledex that sprang open to reveal the numbers of everyone we knew.

Everything stopped when the phone rang. It had to: the cable to the mouthpiece was only two feet long. My nanna would settle herself on the bench seat, wait politely for another three rings to pass, then pick up the handset: 'Good afternoon', she'd say, lips pursed to round her vowels, 'Mrs Thornton speaking.'

She knew rushing down the hallway made one breathless. (And being too eager was crass.)

Calling someone on the Bakelite phone, however, took a seven-year-old's concentration. Dialling the number one was a short stop, so my finger only had to rotate the wheel an inch. But dialling the number nine took effort, a full 240-degree trip. I can still hear the ticka-ticka-ticka as the wheel, reaching the end of the spring, lurched backwards, eager to dislocate my index finger. Mum dialled numbers with the pointy lid of her Bic Cristal pen, the height of secretarial sophistication.

In my teens, the home phone was the centre of my universe. Ours was squat and custard coloured with a panel of ten push-buttons on the front. It had a springy cord that I could stretch from the side table, around the corner and under the pantry door. There I'd sit, out of earshot, between the dog biscuits and the bread bin, phone clamped to my ear, knees hugging my chest. I got leg cramps, but it was worth it. After forty-five minutes on the blower, it was decided – I'd wear my nylon parachute pants on Saturday night.

Sundays were for post-mortems on the electrifying events of the night before:

'Didja see the way he was lookin' at you?'

'As if! Was he *really* lookin' at me?'

'He was lookin' at you, all right!'

'Stoked! Was he lookin' over his shoulder, or right *at* me?'

'Over his shoulder AND right at you!'

'Get off that phone!'

'Gotta go, Mum's doin' her block!'

I'd emerge from the dim-lit pantry, blinking in the daylight.

Back then, I knew all my friends' numbers by heart. Even now, twenty years since my besties moved out of home, I can still rattle off their childhood home numbers, along with my teenage phone patter: 'Hi Mrs Simpson, how are you? Off to the tennis club today? Great! Is Jane there please?'

I cursed holidays that separated me from my home phone. One summer at Rottnest, with heartthrob Andy stranded on the mainland, I spent all my pocket money at the Bathurst settlement pay-phone. It was always occupied. Some bloke with a Swan Gold would be flicking through a tattered White Pages while he leaned against the glass, talking cricket with a mate. I'd wait impatiently as my three-o'clock telephonic rendezvous with Andy drew near. Finally, Swan Gold man would shamble off and I'd dive in, ramming coins into the slot, hoping Andy would pick up, not his Dad.

'Hi Andy! It's me!'

'Hey! Been swimmin'?'

'Yeah. At the Basin.'

'Hot here too. Cricket's on.'

'Oh.'

'Three o'clock tomorrow then?'

'Okay'

'Okay. See ya.'

Now, phone booths are all but extinct. I don't miss them. But watching an old episode of *Dr Who*, my six-year-old son piped up as Tom Baker and his trailing scarf vanished into the Tardis: 'What's that blue box?'

'That's a police booth – a phone booth for policemen.'

I decided the next time we take the kids to Rottnest, I'm going to make a pilgrimage to the Bathurst phone box, that monument to twentieth-century phone technology. (It's still there, outside Unit 501). I'll tell the kids about the time I worked up the nerve to ring a boy I liked, only to slam the phone down in panic as he answered.

And that's the thing with mobiles: they're too delicate. Smart but fragile. I need a phone that can handle my temper when those blasted telemarketers call during dinner. Only the home phone appreciates a good hang up.

MAKE IT OR FAKE IT

I'd never seen a spotted dick up close before. Once as a teenager, I'd seen a picture of one while I was rifling through the miscellany of Mum's third drawer. It was an unappetising sight even in black and white. Mum had written on the top of the cutting in capitals: 'MUST TRY THIS.'

Twenty years later and here was my first spotted dick in the flesh: a cup-sized mound of tea-coloured sponge dotted with currants and swimming in a pool of custard. The waiter slid the plate in front of me with a flourish. That pudding was trying to look exotic, but to me, it was just freckly and dull.

Walking home solo from the restaurant, I wondered if some dishes are social climbers. As a nine-year-old, I thought Mum deliberately matched her canapés to the calibre of her guests. Why else did she serve devils on horseback to the family accountant and angels on horseback to the tennis ladies?

Our long-suffering accountant got half a dozen rashers of bacon, each one rolled up, stuffed with a prune and then grilled until the toothpick caught fire. The tennis ladies had their streaky bacon draped around a creamy clammy oyster.

At gin-and-tonic hour after Wednesday pennants, the tennis ladies (in their fancy pom-pom socks) would arrange themselves in our lounge room. The angels on horseback rode into the good room on a fine-china platter. Keeping steed and saddle in place was a posh toothpick with a frilly top made of coloured cellophane.

Toothpicks were central to 1980s entertaining. Mum made nibbles I liked to call 'traffic lights': a red cocktail onion sitting on a cube of Coon cheese, sitting on a round of Holbrook's gherkin, all three skewered in place by a toothpick. A wooden bowl full of Counter biscuits and an ashtray kept them company.

At dinner parties, she'd serve a tableau of three peeled prawns balanced on the rim of a martini glass. A wedge of avocado lay artfully in the bottom of the glass. In the concave pit where the stone had been, Mum would dollop a dessertspoonful of mayonnaise she'd mixed with a teaspoon of tomato sauce: the required blush-pink lubricant for a *Women's Weekly* prawn cocktail.

Back then, dishes were named after farmyards. *Toad in the hole* was a collection of sausages buried in Yorkshire pudding batter and slathered in onion gravy. At summer barbies, Mum would roll chipolatas in squares of dough and bake them until the pastry puffed up like a doona. Then she'd sashay onto the patio wearing her orange oven mitts and carrying a hot tray. She'd announce: '*Pigs in blankets!*' We kids would throw down our table-tennis bats and come running. Uncle John, who was loud and Scottish, would nudge me and point to the table: 'Sausages in kilts eh! Best you try one of those!' then roar with laughter. I ate a devil on horseback instead.

I had aunties who specialised in mock chicken, mock fish and mock duck. These were dishes that offered themselves up as an animal in disguise. Sometimes I had no clue I'd been deceived. Other times, on the drive home from Aunty Pat's in Roleystone, it only became obvious when Mum remarked: 'Weren't those chicken sandwiches delicious! Who needs a chook!'

Mock duck, however, was for pros like my Great-Aunt Binx. I'd watch her stacking layers of wheat gluten, along with ginger, spices and the liberal use of some powder she called MSG. She'd then marinate her pet project in soy sauce before frying slices in hot oil. I had no idea what the inside of a duck looked like – she didn't need to imitate taste or appearance for my benefit. But I remember being in Thailand and thinking Great-Aunt Binx's mock duck was as good as any quacker I ate in Bangkok.

Mock cream, however, was a travesty. I'd bite into a bakery doughnut expecting the cool richness of cream. Instead, I'd hit a blob of something thick and pasty that glued my tongue to the roof of my mouth. Mock cream couldn't be saved even by jam.

In my teens I discovered certain dinners had mysterious origins no-one wanted to explain. After a week's neglect in the back of the fridge, lamb chops could reinvent themselves as Wakefield chops, a casserole always prepared in secret. I was an adult before I unraveled the secret of the Wakefield chop.

A girlfriend revealed her mum would save a dozen whiffy chops from their rightful destiny in the dustbin. She'd soak them overnight in a conglomerate of sauces (HP, Brown, Worcestershire, soy). After a few hours baking them in the oven, she'd pronounce them: 'Good as new!'

Which brings me to the problem of the dozen snags I bought and forgot last Tuesday. Could I, would I inflict the Wakefield sausage on my family? No. That would be cruel. I'll give them lamb's fry instead.

THE ART OF KEEPING TIME

Memory is a fickle companion. I never know which moments of my life it will choose to preserve. That's why I like to hang on to things – keepsakes – as an antidote to forgetting.

I still have the doll that followed me everywhere as a child. (She was my favourite because she liked to put me first.) I named her Colleen – a good Irish name for a doll made in China. She had turquoise eyes with thick black lashes and strange plastic eyelids that fluttered briefly before closing in forgiveness when I tipped her out of her pram. She also had a blonde cowlick that gave her an unattractive bald spot at the back of her head. But I loved her anyway.

Last week, foraging in the back of a cupboard, I discovered her languishing in a cardboard coffin like Snow White. She was lying on a bed of tissues, wedged into a shoebox – one eye open, one stuck closed – but as lovely as ever. In the bottom of the box was a plastic sleeve containing all the miniature Qantas condiments from my plane trip to Melbourne as a twelve-year-old (salt, pepper, sugar, mustard and my first ever moist towelette). There was also a collection of faded postcards from an uncle with wanderlust and the stub of a concert ticket to Duran Duran in 1983.

Years later, my doll-memory is yet to fail me. I can still remember the embroidered cream flowers on the hem of

Colleen's crimson dress and how her knickers had no elastic. I can recall my twelve-year-old urge to pocket the kangaroo-embossed cutlery on that plane. And I can still picture the euphoric teenage me after Duran Duran emerged from the stage door of the Entertainment Centre and scrawled their initials in my autograph book.

Why cling to such schmaltz? I have kept crates of my relics, rarely opened but dragged from old house to new house, garage to garage. Why do I curate these treasures?

Last month, the pragmatist I live with was cleaning out the carport to make way for eldest son's new ping-pong table. He pushed half a dozen packing boxes towards me: 'It's time', he said, and we both knew what he meant. Inwardly seething (but outwardly compliant), I sat down on an old milk crate and opened my cartons. I pawed through folders stuffed with school exercise books, runner-up tennis trophies and an assortment of papier-mache animals made in Mr Antoine's Year 5 class using strips of newspaper and Clag paste. (Mr Antoine was expert at craft projects but I lived in fear of his sweaty man-hands brushing against mine.)

For the first time since 1993, I ripped the dusty duct tape off a box labelled 'me'. It was stacked with cement-grey Betacam cassettes, an embarrassing archive of my early years of television reportage, when Jana Wendt was my idol. I wore my hair tizzy like hers, with shoulder pads like body armour in my pastel-coloured suits.

Tucked inside a large envelope was a sheath of love letters (mostly mine, unsent). They transported me back to the summer I turned seventeen, adoring the two lifeguards at my local swimming pool. My girlfriend and I would lie artfully reclined on our towels, basting ourselves with Reef Oil. Those lifeguards never came near us. Perhaps because we weren't drowning – or because we looked like two rotisserie chickens crisping in the sun.

And so I tipped out the dregs from the last carton and stuffed our recycling bin with wads of Archie comics and school yearbooks and diaries doodled with love hearts next to names like Scottie and Gav and Craig.

My detritus gone, I felt a pang of despair. Could I mark the passage of time without these mementos? And if these precious souvenirs meant so much to me, why had I spent so little time poring over them?

The next morning, the rubbish truck pulled up and I watched as its robotic arm snatched our bin and dumped my memories amongst its smelly innards. Now the proof of my past was churned up with everyone else's.

I drifted back into the house and surveyed my modernist existence – mass-produced beds and televisions, computers and plates and cups. If a chair breaks, I'll get another one from Ikea. But against the lounge room wall, I saw with fresh eyes my grandmother's sideboard.

That rosewood buffet is the one piece of furniture that wasn't sold off after she died. Instead, it sits in awkward conversation with my sleek new sofa and funky swivelling armchairs. It's a relic of Nan's world, clashing with mine. All the same, I couldn't bear to part with that shellacked showpiece – it's one of the family, like a faithful old dog, following me across suburbs on its unsteady cabriole legs.

Why am I so sentimental about heirlooms I don't much like? Perhaps collecting memories is less about the memories and more about the collecting.

SMALL SATISFACTIONS

HERE'S WHY I'VE GONE TO POT

I have crossed to the dark side. A puddle of shame is staring up at me with eyes like saucers. Actually it is a saucer, because I have given up coffee for tea.

I am well aware that, as I sit with my lovely china cup, I am dangerously close to being cast out as a pariah, that fraternising in coffee shops and ordering a cup of Earl Grey may require a spell in the solitary confinement of a table for one. In Perth apparently, tea cannot match its leaf to the bean.

As the *New York Times* already knew in 1949, coffee is the ultimate 'social binder, a warmer of tongues, a soberer of minds, a stimulant of wit, a foiler of sleep if you want it so'. For many, tea is just a scalding-hot drink, weak in artistry and watery in disposition, requiring pursed lips and too much milling around waiting for the brew to brew.

Coffee, however, is intoxicating, rich and exotic and entices lovers to swoon over its heady aroma. It tastes glorious in the hands of a handsome barista, or equally, a seductive bariste (one who, by repetition alone, has perfected the art of a good pull). Espresso is a notoriously pernickety drink. It demands to be coaxed from the bean at precise temperatures, with air and water in particular measure. Its charm, with deftness of touch, is sublime, and with six-fingered clumsiness, an acrid slop.

I know the great divide in Perth is not between north and south, or the hills and the beaches, it's between those who drink coffee and those who partake of tea. And I know the gulf exists because I see it everywhere. In my frequent travels with pram and small child, I have realised that tea and coffee drinkers inhabit different time zones.

On a Saturday morning when the Tour de Freo arrives back in the 'burbs in a cloud of sweat and caffeine desperation, the pavements outside my favourite cafes are littered with an expensive tangle of bike bling.

Cleats and carbon cast aside, you don't want to get in the way of a peloton of middle-aged lycra converging on the coffee counter to order gallons of flat whites or short blacks. I wonder if they need it as vocal lubricant after long rides, because cup after cup, they mill about gasbagging for hours like old ladies at bridge. (Personally, I stay clear of cyclist queues because once I got jammed up against a gentleman in a codpiece so tight I got an eyeful of his frank and beans before he'd ordered any.)

In my experience, coffee drinkers are always desperate in the morning while tea drinkers, though equally needy, are unusually calm. At that early hour, they wouldn't be seen dead riding anything but side-saddle. Tea drinkers have husbands who bring them a cup of the Queen's best in bed and have pretty cups and mugs and plates of hot buttered toast. I have two lifelong girlfriends who meet me most Friday mornings to discuss the Syrian crisis and how much we weigh, and we wouldn't dream of having coffee – it's tea that fills the space on our plates recently vacated by cake.

And that's another thing – I note from my observations of cafe culture that coffee drinkers don't eat. I suppose they get enough of a kick out of caffeine without needing a chocolate muffin to boot up the day's endorphins. Perhaps it's our Antipodean sensibilities that have demanded we throw off the shackles of penal servitude and dismiss the Blighty's English breakfast variety in favour of the dark continentals?

Italian espresso machines only arrived in the colonies in the 1980s – who would have guessed we would soon have to move our children out of home to make space for them? That said, if you've bought one recently you'd know they cost as much as Guatemala. Ours is a hissing giant on the kitchen bench. Loved to distraction by the caffeine addict in the house, he spent more time researching which one to get than he did on names for his offspring. Either by laziness or design, it leaves a trail of coffee grounds and hot puddles on the bench, presumably to frighten unwitting tea drinkers into giving it a wide berth.

In search of the God shot, namely the perfect espresso, I've had to give up valuable tea-making space. Hence I have eschewed the pot and can no longer bear witness to the 'agony of the leaves'. Aficionados tell me this refers to the unfurling of the tea leaf during steeping and can be quite a dramatic and mesmerising process. I thought the agony of the leaves was having too many deciduous trees in the garden.

Lately, the gossip brimming in tea circles on the internet is that the lowly tea bag rarely contains more than floor sweepings. In fact, is usually a bag of dust. Dust! I live in denial.

There never used to be this rivalry did there? Did coffee always rule in cafe hierarchy? And since when did becoming a barista turn into a career?

My first job was at the once trendy North Cott cafe making cappuccinos on its new-fangled machine. At seventeen years old,

Small Satisfactions

I boiled the milk to within an inch of its life and prided myself on a layer of foam so thick you could stand a surfboard in it.

Later, living in Sydney and working a frenetic pace in television, coffee became a way to live permanently on adrenalin, which all went swimmingly until I was struck down by chest pains. I carted myself off to hospital thinking I was mid-coronary, only to be sternly reprimanded for the heart palpitations brought on by a caffeine overload.

After that I swore off strong coffee and had to drink lattes. Still getting the heart thumps, I returned to Perth in my thirties and resigned myself to drinking decaf, much to the consternation of coffee-house bartenders who couldn't be bothered with such pretence. Even then, it was considered inhumane to force people who had a genuine medical need for coffee to wait in line behind ponces like me who apparently viewed the morning's heart starter as some kind of recreational activity: 'A decaf skim milk latte, please, extra hot, in a mug, not a cup.' I was a coffee toffee, and the laughing stock. So it became tea for me.

I always thought I'd postpone the stately pleasures of the leaf until I, too, was an old lady having a tea break at bingo or sitting down to high tea in stiff whites after lawn bowls. But I can admit here and now, I am an early convert. It's just the thing when the chips are down, and it's always prescribed amidst a scandal. It was the drink that kept the Titanic temporarily afloat, was heavily rationed in World War II as being vital to public morale and it's what Her Majesty ordered with some urgency after being patted on the rear by the Hon. Paul Keating, PM.

So I have decided to be out and proud, and have bought a collection of colourful teacups and saucers to prove this is not a passing fancy. And now I will summon the nerve to rejoin the queue at my favourite corner cafe. I'll shuffle up the line commenting blithely on the weather and if, when it's my turn and I politely request my cup of hot water and dustbag, I hear sniggers or sighs, I will turn to the waiting crowd, stand my ground and declare to all: 'Yes, I'm drinking tea now'. And then I'll add: 'Doctor's orders.'

ENOUGH ABOUT ME

A conversation is not just a rudimentary exchange of information or a conduit for drinking with friends. It has winners and losers. It can be life changing. I know this because a conversation in a pub landed me my husband.

Back then, I didn't know fate had arranged for me to be leaning against the back bar of the Subi hotel with a man wearing Ronnie Barker glasses. He was comfortably stout, like a prized footballer gone to pot, and I noticed his manly hands (I have a thing about extremities). He was charming, disarming and attentive but it was the way he spoke to me that made me skittish, like Bambi. Here was a man who was warming up for a conversational joust. I set out to beguile him with my verbal prowess.

I failed to allow for the first glass of champagne on my empty stomach. It sent my mouth galloping ahead of my brain. Halfway through the second glass, I was babbling and gushing. Sentences I should have filtered for tedium and stupidity dropped straight onto my tongue and became clumsy word spillage. I was all single-entendre, my brilliant wit sabotaged by a bad case of love jitters.

On this night, I thought it best to attempt being a coquette, rather than try to outfox this razor-sharp raconteur when I'd gone all goosey. And anyway, he was asking too many Mensa questions: 'So, being an only child, what have you learnt about other people?'

How to respond? I squirmed. He leaned back and propped his elbows on the bar while a lively silence throbbed between us. My brain darted about in search of a penetrating reply but all I could come up with was: 'The big question for me is why none of my yoga pants have ever been to yoga?'

He grinned – I took it as a compliment. And then he leaned in close, brushed an eyelash off my cheek and whispered 'Make a wish'. I giggled in falsetto.

I secretly asked the champagne fairy for three wishes – I wished this man would take me home and hang his bad tie in my closet, I wished to grow old and grey with him and I wished for thinner arms. The good fairy granted two wishes, and I'm resigned to wearing sleeves.

That is the G-rated version of the night I met my man on a late-summer's night. Our eighth anniversary has just passed (unremarked), but he remains a challenging conversationalist.

Conversation is an art form. We all admire those who have mastered the serve-and-volley of lingual ping-pong.

But some acquaintances suck the oxygen out of the air by talking incessantly. Self-obsession asphyxiates friendships. If I'm buttonholed by a bloke who doesn't draw breath for two minutes, I hightail it to the dessert buffet.

Interrupters also infuriate: my children have perfected the technique. But it's adult interjectors who should be gagged – those people who leap in and ruin my punchlines, or smother me with their preoccupations. I murmur to myself: 'Sorry I was talking while you were interrupting.'

Why can't bores recognise themselves? Some even refer to themselves in the third person, just so we can appreciate them from yet another angle: 'And then the nice girl in Country Road said to me – Barbara Blackwood – you look amazing in that colour. Barbara, that dress goes so well with your tattoo. Barbara, we should name that dress after you – we'll call it… *The Barbara!*'

I, too, used to think my stories were riveting. At twenty, I landed my first job in commercial radio: a chick among peacocks. I answered the phones with try-hard sophistication: '96FM, we will rock you!' Teetering in my white stilettos I would carry cups of International Roast to celebrity disc jockeys with velvet tonsils. On Friday nights I would regale my friends: 'And then he asked me to be the barrel-girl! Me! He told me to giggle and rustle the entry forms so they made crunchy paper noises, it was *sooo* cool…'

Before long I caught two girlfriends rolling their eyes at each other across the table. My ego collapsed. These days I tell my stories while keeping my third eye roving for audience boredom.

Some people like to take over a conversation – they interject about their famous second cousin the soapie extra, or launch into the intricacies of their colonoscopy (scraping the bowels of social convention). Some people feel compelled to convince me that daddy long legs' are poisonous but their mouths aren't big enough to bite people, and if I disagree, they become strident.

At my home in Utopia, my conversational skills are sagging. My twelve-year-old cancels me out with his noise-cancelling headphones. Husband is riveted by *The Footy Show* and can't be distracted, so my three-year-old and I compete for each other's attention.

Small Satisfactions

Sometimes, when I want to ask my beloved about the state of our relationship, I'll sidle up to him and say: 'Honey, do you remember that night we met in that pub?' And he'll smile and say: 'Yes, Blossom, that's the night you thought talking about yourself constituted a conversation.'

HERE'S TO HAND-ME-DOWN HAND-WRITING!

Memory has a mind of its own. At random, it chooses what to keep. My grandmother's handwriting is writ large in my memory. I remember her ringing me on her black Bakelite phone: 'I've posted you a surprise, darling.' She knew my little legs would be dashing to the front gate every five minutes to see if the postie was a speck up the road.

I could pick out my nan's penmanship in an instant, even before the perfumed envelope gave it away. Her capitals had graceful loops and flourishes – an artistic hand that also embroidered daisies on dresses for my doll. I watched mesmerised as the same hand whisked eggs into a blur to make dainty sponges.

It was there, in my nan's kitchen, that she wrote me her shopping lists: long columns of her handwriting showing off her beautiful curlicue C for corned beef – 1 lb. Potatoes with a flouncy P, a firm downstroke for the B in Bovril, an exaggerated T for treacle and Sago – the o with a hook that swept the next word 'Pudding' into brackets – so I'd know what Sago was for. Such foreign-sounding things she wanted. I tucked her list into my koala purse and pedalled to the shop. First hurdle: deciphering her script. Second hurdle: matching the groceries to the strange words on the list. Then I'd ride home with bulging string bags hanging from my handlebars, banging on my knees or swinging dangerously into the spokes.

Even now, her writing goes hand-in-hand with how I remember her: graceful and neat. She left behind that permanent imprint of her ninety years on the planet. My nan's lovely cursive resides on the backs of family photos. It lives inside the letters we keep as treasures under the lid of the piano stool at Mum's house. The seat of our family.

My own handwriting is as erratic as a chicken scratch. I'm so out of practice I can barely jot down half a page without getting writer's cramp. I used to write my television stories long-hand on spiral notebooks, a welter of script. I sweated on the fire-escape stairs outside the newsroom, scribbling away as deadline approached. Sentences that didn't sound right when spoken aloud were roughly scrubbed out in favour of rhythmic ones. Sudden brainwaves would force themselves onto the pad, squeezed into margins – a scrawl legible only to me. It was always a race to see whether inspired thoughts would vaporise before I could get them on paper.

No such trouble now. My laptop and I are intimates. My fingers fly over the keys – brain and hands finally in unison. Typing fast feels masterly. With such mechanical clarity, should I ever bother with pens?

My children won't remember life before the internet. Their ideas will be pressed onto paper by the clicking of keys rather than the scratching of biros. For them, postcards will be quaint reminders of holidays before Facebook.

In high school French I decided my number seven needed the European sophistication of a cross bar. I was a maths dunce but with one horizontal stroke, I became numerically glamorous

– those sevens of mine were so continental they could have been smoking Gauloises and eating croissants. Smitten, I have written my sevens with a bar ever since: seventh heaven!

As classmates, we took great pains to graffiti our fanciest handiwork all over each others' diaries. We changed our writing styles as often as the hems on our pleated beige dresses. Even now, I can instantly picture the cursive of my closest school friends: all those birthday cards and books gifted with their funny, affectionate inscriptions.

Curious, I don't know the handwriting of newer friends. We talk and text and email, but don't pen notes. Will their writing be bold or slapdash or in beautiful italics? Are they right-handed or mollydooker? I'd like to know.

My husband hides a handwritten note each time he creeps out of the house at dawn for the airport. I wake up in our bed and feel less empty for the small thrill of finding his letter. Usually it's tucked under my laptop or in the Cornflakes box. Silly I know, but it's comforting to see the essence of him on paper, a billet-doux tiding me over until his return. I return the favour by planting an even more effusive love letter in his suitcase. (I usually wrap it around nasty household bills, each one annotated with a love heart in the hope he'll pay them and leave me flush with cash.)

Now I'm mourning a graceful skill that has had its day. Handwriting is an art because expressing ourselves in ink is an exercise in restraint. Even a rude letter starts with 'Dear...' before roasting the recipient. How many times have I dashed off an email forgetting my hasty reply might be mistaken for bluntness – I'm always embarrassed at sounding impolite. Perhaps I need to slow down and reacquaint myself with the gentleness of handwriting. If I concentrate, I might even be able to make it legible.

SHH! SAY IT IN A WHISKER

It's lucky beards don't hold grudges because I make damning generalisations about their owners. Shifty weak-chinned buggers they are. I like to know where the beard ends and the man begins. Why the wearers of crumb-catchers always stroke their whiskers while thinking about what they're hiding behind.

I've had some bad run-ins with beards. It started in the 1970s with Catweazle, the TV wizard. I watched every episode from behind a beanbag, revelling in being scared witless. I don't know if it was Catweazle's ratty goatee, the crazed look in his eyes or that toad he kept in the pocket of his filthy brown cloak, but that warlock did some lasting damage. Beards gave me the heebie-jeebies.

I turned the corner in Year 6. My teacher Mr Pearsall had an Abraham Lincoln beard, bushy but neatly clipped and a vibrant shade of orange. In the afternoons, he sat on a stool reading to us from a book called *Stranger from the Depths,* a gripping novel about a bunch of kids who befriend an underwater alien. As he spoke, his beard would catch the sunlight streaming in through the windows of our demountable classroom. His face aglow, Mr Pearsall and his incandescent beard were mesmerising. That book came to life in the hands of a man who might well have been an alien himself.

Small Satisfactions

I never quite understood the appeal of the beard; why ninety-eight per cent of the world's lumberjacks, sea captains and bikies are so attached to their woolly faces. But then I met Gordon.

Gordon and his wife live not far from us. Their Jack Russell and my three-year old like a morning constitutional so we always stop to chat. I'm fascinated by Gordon's wispy white beard, the way it fans out from his chin then tapers to a point halfway down his chest.

Even the slightest breeze lifts the delicate ends of his beard and they float up around his face. Abstractedly, he gently strokes them down: 'Fifty years I've had it now', he tells me, 'Grew it at thirty. Every day I comb it, shampoo it once a week. I used to plait it to keep it out of the way, or roll it up and pin it with a clip under my chin, but I'm a fading hippie now so it can fly free.'

His wife shrugs: 'I still don't like it', and Gordon roars with laughter. I suggest he might like to reacquaint himself with the bottom half of his face just to keep the missus happy. He gives his beard a pat and replies: 'Nope, too late. It's part of me.'

My razor-sharp spouse likes to grow a beard on holidays. He calls it a beard but really it's just ginger scraggle. After two weeks it's like a badly mown lawn – tufts growing east on one cheek, south on the other, a prickly clump on his chin sporting a smear of dried toothpaste.

But that scruff of whiskers has a strange effect on him. Newly hirsute, he fancies himself as Chuck Norris. I play along and declare him the most macho bloke. And then the bearded one kisses me like he's Lone Wolf McQuade and days later I'm still applying ointment to my gravel rash.

Small Satisfactions

This season's footballers aren't doing facial hair any favours either. Those bushrangers just make the game more untidy. I say leave the chin curtains where they belong, boys: in the 1970s – on singers like Kenny Rogers and Barry Gibb.

But certain beards have the ability to stop traffic. Only yesterday, catching up with two pals at a coffee shop, one girlfriend exclaimed 'Hey! Check out that beard!'. We all turned to look outside and there was an old gent with a giant Father Christmas beard, white and bushy with an elaborate moustache that curled up at the ends, giving the illusion of a permanent smile.

On older men, the beard can add a veneer of gravitas, on younger men, a rugged virility. Or villainy: Fu Manchu's evil moustache became the template for Disney scoundrels and Hollywood's bad guys.

Whatever the fashion, I say Brad Pitt's untamed goatee looks one park bench away from deranged. George Clooney's salt-and-pepper version gives him the kind of retrosexual manliness my mum fancies.

These days, facial hair needs lessons in etiquette. A beard is too big if you can wring it out, or it joins up with the hair on your chest. A beard must not be used as a bib for eating garlic prawns. When two beards cross paths, the bigger one gets right of way.

None of this matters in our house. Yesterday morning, as Mr seven-o'clock-shadow lathered up, I commiserated that the beard-growing season doesn't start until Christmas: 'Never mind', I said 'you look just as rugged without one.' 'That's nice, Blossom, because I haven't had a close shave in years. Maybe you could find me a razor that hasn't shaved the beard off your legs.'

MAKING SCENTS OF LIFE

We were trapped. Sealed in a lift that was ripe with the stench of unwashed human. That malodorous cloud was a parting gift from the previous occupant. We spluttered out at the nineth floor. 'What was that stink?' asked my twelve-year-old. 'That', I said, 'was some serious B-O.'

I can bring to mind a handful of occasions (mostly in aeroplanes) when I have flinched at the smell of another human being. Yet the faint milky sweetness of a baby's head is intoxicating. I want to drink it in, inhale the newness and neediness of life. The musky scent of my husband is the smell of belonging — me to him — comforting and arousing at the same time.

At my supermarket, it's frustrating trying to sniff out a new-season's peach when peachiness has been turned frigid by cold storage. I see why people are embracing farmers markets as an open-air feast for the senses. A home-grown tomato smells of the sun. It's a revelation after shop-bought tomatoes whose scent has been all but snuffed out.

Sometimes it takes a conscious effort to be reacquainted with the persuasive power of scent. Coming home minus kids from school this morning I stopped in the park, underneath the Norfolk Island pines. What does the wind smell like? I'd never considered it before. My nose could detect something familiar and then, with a rush, I realised what it was: I was smelling the heat rising off grass sprinkled with needles. Warm currents of air on their way to thirty-nine degrees that had sucked up the scent of pine and grass clippings. I could distil the essence of that February morning far more by the smell of the wind than by the sight of the big pines or the familiar screeches of the white cockatoos. I tried all morning to recall the scent of that warm breeze, but the memory faded as the day wore on.

Smells are the easiest and hardest things to remember. My grandmother's white Morris 1100 retained its new-car bouquet for twenty years. Try as I might, I cannot bring to mind that favourite scent. My brain offers me visual reminders instead – the cherry-red of the vinyl bench seats and my nanna at the wheel with her pink powdered cheeks and a harlequin-print polyester dress. Perhaps smell doesn't like to work alone. Perhaps memories of smells erode with time or are muddied by subsequent layers of living.

The twentieth century French writer Marcel Proust believed some memories are imprinted more firmly than others by their smell. He wrote of a man overwhelmed by his sudden ability to recall, in vivid detail, the madeleine cakes he once dipped in his tea as a child. My grandmother's Morris is my Proustian biscuit. Except I've never quite managed to capture the essence of that delicious scent.

The internet and smart phones have eroded my senses. The Internet has changed the way I shop for a birthday cake and how I order the frangipani for the back garden. Where once I was driving to the patisserie and swooning over the thick buttery fumes of so much cake, or gliding around a nursery exhilarated by the perfume of so many blossoms, now I am pressing keys on a computer with my sense of smell in hibernation. No need for it: at my desk I am scentless. ('Senseless more like it', suggests the cynic from the sofa.) I tell you, technology smells of nothing. It is sterile.

Unlike junk email, odours cannot be fended off with a delete button. They don't wait to be invited and they like to hang about (bad smells have no manners). Prawn heads in the sun, too much fresh paint, big Jersey cows trampling their manure at the Royal Show. As a child, I wished the reek of so much animal wouldn't overpower the delicate waft of spun sugar from the fairy floss stand.

I'm fussy about smells so it's just as well I'm woman, not dog. If the sniffing power of a beagle is 100,000 times greater than mine, no wonder he loves to jam his snout against the rear of every dog he meets. That must be the same kind of rush I'd get riding the Magic Mountain at Disneyland. (Only a canine lover can stand the smell of wet dog.)

For me, the most perplexing smell comes as I open my front door after holidays away from home. In those first few seconds of walking inside I suddenly register what my homelife must smell like. It's as though my nose needs reminding which house it belongs to. For a split second, I am a stranger to my own scent. And then it vanishes, replaced by the familiar sound of my footsteps down the hall.

There are scents I could drown in, float away on, never tire of: the smell of a child's warm breath as you carry him asleep from the car to his bed, the nape of my daughter's neck after her bath. Gingerbread baking before Christmas. Peeling oranges, the fragrance of my mum's Oil of Olay as she braided my hair before school. These are the smells precious to a life.

Perhaps memory has designed these smells to be recalled piecemeal, never whole. I can think of no finer way to protect their potency.

TRIPPING DOWN MEMORY LAME

I have been cursed with forgetting. I forget new names and old acquaintances. I forget what people do and who they're doing it with. I have sudden panics at the supermarket when a face I know (attached to a name I don't) stops me at the fish counter: 'How are you? It's been ages! Have you seen any of the gang lately?'

Gang? With rising panic, I point to the seafood display and launch headlong into an embarrassing non sequitur: 'No, I haven't seen the gang lately, but hey! Have you ever seen such sad little prawns, I bet they got bullied at school for being shrimps!' Good grief! – I keep up this moronic prattle whilst simultaneously pleading with my brain to please, please deliver the name of this person. Then at least I can spare her (and me) the agony of my tediously inane small talk.

Suddenly the penny drops and I blurt out: 'So, Penny! How are the girls at Pilates?' Gotcha! The relief is instant. For the next thirty seconds I say Penny's name in every sentence. Our conversation becomes the festival of Penny from Pilates. She seems pleased. Penny and I part ways with a girly kiss and I promise to go to class more than once a month. As I walk back to the car, I begin a mantra of repeating her name over and over in my head. I pray 'Penny from Pilates' sticks firmly in there somewhere for next time.

Small Satisfactions

I've always been conversationally absent-minded. But I'm getting worse after four decades of meeting people. What if my forgetting is laziness? What if I am just not paying enough attention to what people tell me?

Would it be less awkward to admit: 'I'm really sorry, but who are you and how do you fit into my life?' But then I realise I'm not ready to be a social pariah.

I have the same problem with reading. My book collection is a vast catalogue of forgetting. I was enthralled by *Cloudstreet* yet retained virtually nothing of the experience. I can give you a line about the plot (neighbours) and the locale (West Leederville, wasn't it?). Maybe a character's name if I'm lucky (Rose Pickles?). But my affection for *Cloudstreet* is nothing more memorable than a warm feeling. Ask me about books I've devoured and all I can give you is a vague idea of a story 'liked', 'loved' or 'hated'.

Forgetting has consequences for my vanity, too. Deep in conversation with someone cleverer than me, I'm holding my own nicely when suddenly, I'm unable to pluck the word I need from the left side of my head. Inwardly cursing, outwardly stammering, my unfinished sentence hangs in the air. My listener kindly tries to fill the awkward silence by changing the subject, but our conversation has lost its momentum and lurches to an uncomfortable end. We make our excuses, and I slink away, mortified.

Yet I can reel off reams of useless trivia, without even trying. I can recall watching a documentary that said Charlie Chaplin once entered as himself in a look-alike competition and came third. I can tell you that no matter how high you throw an egg, it will never break if it lands on grass. (We just tried it at the park.) I can remember my school project from Year 5 revealing cows have no front teeth. And I know no-one can lick their elbow.

But can I remember to dress my six-year-old lad in a beret and moustache for school French day? Nope. And that's after reading the note from his teacher a fortnight ago and writing a reminder in big red letters in my diary. Let's just say I forgot to check my diary. A small boy rolled up to school in his regulation blue shorts and white shirt to be met by a crowd of petits enfants oozing Gallic charm. I made a mad dash home to fetch sobbing child a stripy Breton shirt and a jaunty knotted scarf and missed my Pilates class with Penny.

Lately I seem to be unable to picture my children as babies. This frustration is particularly acute with my eldest. As a toddler, I knew every dimple and freckle on his little face by heart. I thought I would never forget the sight of him crawling commando down the hallway. Or how at age five, he would slurp jelly through the two-finger gap in his teeth. Now I can only summon the thirteen years of memories by consulting photographs or watching old home movies. My mind will not reproduce even the things dearest to me.

Is there a remedy for forgetfulness? I'm yet to find it, though I know paragons of memory who swear by Sudoku and crosswords. And bridge. The closest I've come to mentally stimulating card games is Strip Jack Poker. Come to think of it, I've never forgotten anyone I played that with.

BEEN THERE, DONE THAT

For six years I have existed in a wasteland of sodden tea leaves and limp, spent teabags. Coffee and I parted ways over heart palpitations and the jitters. Even so, it was a bitter breakup: doctor's orders.

At cafes, I now endure the taunts of coffee-drinking friends: 'Tea? Really? (Smirk) Okay – water in a cup for her. I'll have a skinny double-shot, extra-hot, flat white, in a takeaway cup.'

Coffee snobbery is rife amongst Perth poseurs. At my local coffee house, my delicate teacup and saucer signposts me as persona non grata. Apparently, I take up too much space at the pocket-sized tables with my collection of dinky pots (one for hot water) and my jug of frigid milk.

I have but one ally who shares my disdain for coffee snobs: a lawyer no less (and a tea-totaller to boot). Emboldened by the promise of anonymity, he sounded off at a recent poolside barbecue: 'Coffee addicts are an unholy alliance between heroin junkies and wine snobs. Of course, they mask their sad dependence by acting self-righteous and superior. But we non-coffee-drinkers are very tolerant people.' (His wife took me behind a palm tree to say: 'He thinks he's a small-L liberal, but really he's a big-F fascist').

Small Satisfactions

Cafe society has its own pecking order and tea-drinkers are its eccentrics. Coffee purists would rather we Mad Hatters fraternised amongst ourselves out of sight. They would prefer we took tea at home in our Wonderlands resplendent with knitted tea cosies, Wedgewood china and silver spoons. That's where time stands still and it's never too late for a cuppa tea.

My husband, too, is a smug caffeine addict. At work, he'll schlep up and down St Georges Terrace in pursuit of his preferred barista. Town baristas have cult followings. My husband's current favourite has a nose ring and a front mullet (ristretto drinkers call that a frollet). Last I heard, that hairy barista and his coffee machine were operating to wide acclaim from a hole in a wall in London Court (brick dust makes the coffee taste authentically Columbian).

I tell you this because I like to practice hypocrisy. Last week, as my tea-rista filled my pot with steaming water, he leaned conspiratorially across the counter: 'Don't you miss coffee?'

I went blank. Then I weaved my way back to my table juggling my saucer and rattling cup in one hand – teapot and milk jug in the other. Boiling water dripped onto my big toe. I jumped, and my spoon clattered to the floor: a flotilla of heads jerked up from their macchiatos and skinny lattes and their rivetting coffee-enhanced conversations.

Under the scutiny of that cafe crowd, I had an epiphany: I did miss coffee! I missed being dark and dangerous and brooding. I missed sneering at tea-drinking fools. I retraced my steps to the counter and announced: 'Okay, Alberto, I surrender! Gimme me a weak flat white.'

He winked at me and belted his last puck of spent coffee grounds into the knockbox: 'One lukewarm milkshake for the

Small Satisfactions

born-again coffee virgin coming right up!' The businessman at my elbow snickered.

Within an hour of that coffee, my single entendres had doubled. My brain was Stephen Hawkingly-alert. I began reciting TS Eliot in my head. I decided I too, could measure out my life in coffee spoons. And then I drifted home in a daze of caffeine euphoria.

My renewed infatuation with coffee has caused some consternation at home. My husband now has to share his prized coffee machine. Some mornings, I catastrophise that he loves that coffee machine more than me.

My husband is fastidious about his morning brew. He's obsessed with the surgical cleaning of his beloved contraption. Most mornings this week, he has beckoned me from my lukewarm milkshake to lecture me on why I should be grateful to have a threesome with his machine.

He gruffly points out the trail of coffee grounds across the kitchen bench. He gets down on his hands and knees to demonstrate how they have spilled onto the floor and made it gritty. He accuses me of not wiping the dark orifice where the groupo attaches to the machine. (Only coffee nerds could come up with a name like groupo for a metal filter with a handle.) He says I haven't scraped the last deflated bubble of dried milk from the frothing proboscis. (I too, can up with stupid names for ordinary things.)

To avert a serious domestic, I promise him I'll be more respectful of the coffee ritual. I slink back to my sweet warm pudding of a drink and force myself to think sweet warm thoughts about my man.

And then I have another epiphany: Hang on! We're on

the same side! I am once again a coffee addict. That makes me one of the in-crowd. Coffee makes me invincible. It's time we high-borns showed those ridiculous tea-types who's boss.

BUGBEARS

SMOKES AND MIRRORS

Smoking was my religion once. I worshipped at the altar of Benson & Hedges. I was convinced that slim gold box had a certain prestige that would rub off on me. It didn't, but I kept smoking anyway. That was until I discovered Sobranie cocktail cigarettes and was smitten with the idea of matching my lavender dress to my lavender cigarette.

In the 1980s, Sobranies had gold filters and came in rainbow colours like a (flammable) box of crayons. At nineteen, a girlfriend and I, going to a ball, split our waitressing money to buy a pack so she could match the turquoise Sobranies to her eyes. I thought those coloured cigarettes gave me what the French call panache: a combination of charisma and reckless courage. But all they really gave me were head spins and a throat made of sandpaper.

I was sure it was the tobacco haze that gave smokers their air of worldly sophistication. I desperately wanted membership to their club. At parties, the nonsmokers stayed warm (and dull) inside, while the smokers gathered in conspiratorial huddles on the verandah, laughing at their in-jokes and admiring each other's magnetic personalities.

Inhaling burnt leaves was fundamentally unpleasant but I persevered, fearful of being labelled a wowser. Before long, I discovered a lit cigarette became a smoke signal luring interesting people my way. 'Got a light?' was the password to smoking solidarity between strangers. No matter where we came from, we had our addiction in common.

I thought boys liked girls who smoked. One night at the pub, I watched a girl sidle up to a group of blokes. She leaned in provocatively, dangling an unlit cigarette between her ballerina fingers. The conversation evaporated. Those four lads couldn't extract their lighters fast enough. Four zippos burst into life as their owners jostled to anoint the young lady. When I passed in front of her ten minutes later I realised her male entourage was more enthralled by her high beams and low singlet than by her smoking prowess.

Radio bred serious smokers. Aged twenty-one, my first newsroom was a glassed cage where plumes of smoke spiralled from ashtrays like genies from lanterns. Old hands smoked while they read the news – cigarette in one hand, script in the other. The new-girl cadet decided smoking might give her some journalistic cachet. I joined the A-grade smokers and lit up at 6 am. By the end of a breakfast shift, our overflowing ashtrays were ranked in order of effort. My boss, Murray Dickson, always beat me by a packet.

Back then, choosing a brand was like choosing a footy team: would it be Dunhills, Alpines or Kents? No woman ever smoked Camels. No man smoked menthols. A man's man smoked Marlboro Reds, Peter Stuyvesants or rolled his own, one-handed, while driving a semi-trailer. Brickies dragged on their Winnie Blues and wolf-whistled from scaffolding. (I felt indignant and self-conscious, but if it happened tomorrow, I'd be thrilled.)

Bugbears

No-one told me I could betray my brand without being charged with treason. I worked out that I could smoke John Player Specials one week and Sterling Special Milds the next. In London, I joined the pallid crowd and bought Marlboro Lights. In the early 1990s I settled on Benson & Hedges and dedicated myself to a decade of nicotine addiction.

At family dinners, I thought I could slip outside for a dozen quick puffs and no-one would notice. I'd bury the stub in the potted palm by Mum's front door. Then I'd sneak into the bathroom and perform a surgical hand scrub before brushing my teeth and rejoining the table. I thought a smear of toothpaste could mask the stench of tobacco embedded in my clothes and hair. Who did I fool? Just me. How on earth did nonsmokers put up with us?

I can remember when pop-out ashtrays were built into seats on buses, in cinemas and on planes. What an outcry there was when gutsy politicians banned smoking in pubs and restaurants! But for me, smoking had become robotic. I despised my foul habit but it owned me. One by one, friends were giving up but I was the straggler who deluded herself by declaring she still enjoyed it.

Once, on an Air France flight in 1997, I wandered through the ash-coloured curtains into the smoking section. I found myself sandwiched between four Japanese chain-smokers while I waited for the loo. Our toes almost touching, they exhaled their smoke over each other's shoulders. No-one spoke. Stale fumes thickened the air, but those men stood puffing away for most of the flight. I realised I didn't even need to light up. I could just inhale.

Many times I tried and failed to quit. Common sense and willpower eventually triumphed over my ten-a-day stupidity.

(On weekends, I didn't count.) Giving up was just as well, really because you recall that potted palm outside Mum's front door? The one I liked to use as an ashtray?

    It died.

THE POLITENESS POLICE DON'T NEED A BADGE

At my neighbourhood cafe, social order is upheld by the good breeding of its customers. Crass, rude, ignorant oafs are not tolerated here. Customers know to walk outside to answer their mobiles. The discourteous cop withering stares for jumping the coffee queue. We're the bad manners police: we catch and kill our own.

Last Thursday morning, my curiosity got the better of me and I asked my friendly barista: 'Where's the baby?'

He was puzzled too. A newborn's cry, high-pitched and grating, filled the cafe. It had the familiar staccato rhythm of all distressed babies: that frenzied pattern of hoarse barks that pains a mother's ears and lodges in her gut. We both began scanning the tables. I couldn't see any baby capsules tucked beside chair legs. No anxious mums were tending prams on the footpath. That newborn wail drowned out the cafe music and stopped conversation. 'Where's it coming from?' called a middle-aged woman sitting by the wall.

'Is it coming from the kitchen?' offered two young girls in the corner. The barista left his burbling machine to check. I wandered back to my table with my tea, still casting about for the howler. The only customers who didn't seem perturbed were a grandma and grandpa, trying to keep a toddler entertained with a biscuit and their mobile phone.

The waitress was the first to zero in on the distress cry. It was coming from the grandma's phone: she was playing the toddler a video – presumably of the newest baby in the family.

'Excuse me', the waitress said, 'but your phone is disturbing our customers. Would you mind turning it down?'

'Oh for goodness sake!' said the grandma, immediately taking offence. 'It's not loud. Don't be ridiculous!'

'Well, it's louder than our music and it's upsetting our customers', the waitress replied. 'Could you please turn it down?'

The grandma grunted towards her husband, then scooped up her belongings. She grabbed the toddler by the hand, scraped a chair out of the way and barged out the door.

We all exchanged quizzical looks and tut-tutted over the drama. The grandma with the loud phone had been disciplined for the common good. Cafe society resumed with a round-table discussion on civil niceties.

Sometimes, even small discourtesies are infuriating. I shake my head in disbelief when drivers refuse to let me merge. I glower at people who sidle into the middle of my line at the checkout. And I'm always appalled at the rudeness of customers who expect to be served first, having arrived last. When confronted by the arrogant or self-righteous rule-breaker, I feel compelled to mete out some small measure of punishment: a dirty look, a cutting remark. But I rarely give in to the impulse to mouth off: for some reason I don't feel old enough.

On a rare outing to the cinema last week, I sat behind a nerdy bloke who gave me (and everyone within a three-row radius) a running commentary on the merits and lineage of Apple computers. It was a pointless exercise given we were watching the biopic about Steve Jobs. For several minutes, we listened to the boorish prattle from computer nerd, row G, until a businessman sitting next to me clenched his teeth and delivered a loud: 'Shhh!'

Being an obnoxious kind of nerd, the row G loudmouth continued his critique until a gravelly voice from somewhere behind me exploded: 'Quiet! Or I'll have you thrown out!'

A sea of heads swivelled on rubbernecks and several of us clapped our appreciation. One man had enforced cinema's first commandment: Do not speak above a whisper. (Better still, do not speak at all.) The nerd in row G fell silent. Social order had been restored.

I was a public nuisance once. Aged twenty-one, I would drive my flatmate from Scarborough to the city, where we both worked. Running late as always, we'd hit Powis street and groan. In the right-hand lane, waiting to turn onto the freeway were cars queued 100 metres back from the on-ramp. So I would hoon up the inside lane to the front of the queue. There, I'd stop dead, and snap on my indicator. At the slightest gap, I'd nudge my way into the turn lane and in front of whichever poor sod had been inching patiently forwards. Whooping with delight, I'd theatrically wave my thanks in my rear view mirror and speed onto the freeway. Usually, the driver behind would throw up his hands in contempt. I would feel a moment's guilt and then a rush of adrenalin for pulling off yet another peak-hour coup.

This became a daily infraction – my girlfriend would cover her face with her hands and cringe: 'I can't look! Tell me when it's over!' Even now I'm amazed at my rudeness. (Back then, I called it ingenuity.)

As a reformed rule-breaker who's now a stickler for manners, I'm ready to atone for my driving sins. So next time I cut you off on the freeway, I won't be the slightest bit offended when you overtake me and shout through your window: 'Moron! Are you blind?!'

Minus glasses, I am blind, but I guess that's not what you're driving at.

CONFESSIONS FROM A PAIR OF LOSERS

In our house, I am the finder of lost things. Except if the lost thing is the repair kit for the coffee machine. Sealed in a plastic bag, these are special tools: a weird-looking tube and a yellow brush, a metal thingy with a hole punctured at one end and a perforated paper cone.

They are also implements so vital to the espresso-making process that I've never seen them before. My husband says otherwise, seeing as it's me who has lost them.

Three weeks ago, as I was making beds, our Breville coffee machine began gurgling uncomfortably. As it choked down the last of the Costa Rican Arabicas, my newly woken (de-caffeinated) husband yelped from the kitchen. I ran to his side. We stood by the coffee machine, helpless. It shook uncontrollably, then exhaled a weak steamy breath and was still. I thought I heard a faint death rattle in its metal throat, then silence. With no trace of emotion my husband turned to me: 'Quick – get the cleaning bag, the coffee machine's croaked.'

The bag wasn't hiding in the big red bowl on the kitchen bench kept precisely for mystery objects. Nor was it at the bottom of the pantry, or in the garage (you never know). For three days in a row, my husband drove at sunrise the 200 metres to the corner cafe to satisfy his craving. On his return, only slightly less agitated, he demanded: 'Find the damn repair kit, Blossom.' And so my hunt began anew.

Clearly my powers of encyclopedic placement had let me down. All that memorising of the precise whereabouts of each item belonging to five people in one house had come to nothing. Suddenly one see-through zip-lock bag was as lost as eighteen minutes of Watergate tape.

However, I did find the allen key for dismantling the spare bed, the commemorative gold coin we got sucked into buying at the Bell Tower and an unclaimed Medicare receipt from 2011.

In our family, there are two types of searches for lost things: there is a 'boy look' and a 'girl look'. When the man of the house misplaces the keys to his ute, he swivels his head from left to right before announcing: 'Nup, they're not here.'

This constitutes a 'boy look.' It does not involve looking under or behind things or anywhere above or below eye level.

My bloke, when desperate, will ramp up a 'boy look' by taking one step in each direction from the kitchen bench before accusing: 'What have you done with my keys!'

That's when I can swoop in for a 'girl look'. I shift sheaths of unpaid Telstra bills to their rightful file and drawer and put magazines with Ray Martin on the cover into the recycling at last. I clear my husband's desk of stretched-out paper clips, discarded envelopes and a pagoda of Post-it notes. Along the way I also find eldest son's missing pocketknife and joy! – the plug for the bath.

Eventually I discover the ute's keys chilling on the third shelf of the fridge: 'Oooh, that's right!' he says, 'I put them on that six-pack so I wouldn't forget the beers.'

Bugbears

'Girl looks' are imperative when living with teenage boys. My man-child can't remember what day it is, let alone where he put his lunch box: actually nowhere. It's still in his school bag on the porch, lid off, with a few crusts and a whiffy yoghurt container signposting a free meal for passing vermin.

Sometimes it's me that feels like the lost thing – picking my way through the jumble of other people's stuff trying to restore order – no place for me. My carefree days are behind me, but I'm not yet old enough to need taking care of. Instead, I am sitting uncomfortably in the embrace of middle age – needed instantly when tummies are hungry or sock drawers need a refill. Why can't I be wanted as much as needed?

I like to pretend I know where everything is. Even the children. And if something is too important to lose, I put it in the only place I'm guaranteed to find it: my bra. Recently, while having a (womanly) check-up, my doctor said: 'Pop up here on the bed and take off your bra and we'll be done in no time.' So I unsnapped my bra and a train ticket, two one-dollar coins and the lens cap for my camera dropped onto the floor. (Best to take photos dressed in something with pockets.)

So now a month has passed and a new repair kit has been delivered: $68.95. The coffee machine has spluttered back to life and the household is re-caffeinated by 7 am.

But last night I had a dream, a dream so real I woke up and my brain was instantly alert. Suddenly, I remembered where I'd put that indispensable zip-lock bag with all the coffee parts: in the bin. The same place I put all useless-looking tubes, metal-thingies and strange paper cones. But that's a guilty secret best left between you and me.

MYTHS OF A CLASSLESS SOCIETY

A pedigree is no longer something you're just born with. It can be learnt, earned, inherited, pretended. Perhaps that's why class is still such a touchy subject: no-one really knows how the class system works anymore.

Most of us claim to be middle class, except few of us really know what 'middle class' means. It can mean poor, but with credit cards. Or it can mean wealthy, but with working-class values.

I have a friend, a top-notch lawyer, who declares he'll always be blue collar at heart. He says he pines for well-behaved children, a respectful wife, humble sports stars, union leaders who don't lie and Labor politicians who care about the hoi polloi. (He also keeps a fluoro safety vest in the wine cellar in case he ever has to change a light globe.)

Middle class is now a destination: those who claim it stretch from the highly privileged (people who would never call themselves 'rich' in public) to families paying off the two-year loans on their home theatres and iPads. Middle-class people tout their disposable income, even if they relentlessly dispose of it.

Why do so many now aspire to be called 'middle class?' Does the class struggle no longer exist? Of course, we're all equal now – how nice! I guess that means 'working class' has become a dirty word? It used to be worn as a badge of honour – a respectable way to earn a quid with your muscles. Skill with a shovel distinguished real blokes from pen-pushers, construction brawn from the soft-skinned and the un-tanned.

Luckily for me, journalism is rarely choosy about the social standing of its recruits. In television, the gift of the gab and an ear for storytelling are prized whether you were born rich or grew up on welfare cheques. And those who hailed from out in the sticks often had the common touch – that ability to make people feel so at ease, they willingly poured out their stories and then asked: 'Would you like to stay for tea?'

Politicians target us like we're some bland mass of supplicants. We're not. Take that hackneyed Labor line 'working families' – it has been trotted out *ad nauseam* for the past five years. Politicians imagine we'll swallow rhetoric like 'working families' because the phrase appeals to blue- and white-collar workers alike. Actually, it's a cliché that makes even the well-to-do feel included.

The mining boom has been a wonderful leveller. It has enabled the unskilled, tradies and construction blokes (and gals) to set themselves up for life. But if you ever needed proof that high society doesn't tolerate upstarts, then the mindless label 'cashed-up bogan' says it all. Poseurs looks upon the nouveau riche as a blight on the social landscape – as an unwelcome species who carve up the genteel tranquillity of waterfront living with their jet skis and oversized runabouts.

Even the *Wall Street Journal* swooped in for a closer look at Australia's new money when it unearthed a twenty-five-year-old high-school drop-out from Mandurah who was earning $208,000 a year as a long-hole driller up north. He happily admitted to blowing every cent he earned on his Chevy ute, custom bikes, electronic gadgetry and partying: 'Without mining, I'd be an auto mechanic making $600 a week. I love mining, mate.'

Blue-collar workers have become a precious commodity in this country – rarely has manual labour been in such demand. Who's not fascinated by a resources boom that has driven wages into hyperdrive? But why isn't a forex trader with a Ferrari a cashed-up bogan too? Only the working class cop it for daring to rise above their station. Perhaps Australia's middle is uncomfortable about relying on mine workers to keep the economy afloat by splurging their red-dusted pay cheques.

Urban myth would have us believe every frustrated shophand and salesman has packed it in and headed north to drive a dump truck for $150K. That's a flight of imagination, not a Skywest flight to Paraburdoo. A cashed-up bogan might be the much lampooned poster-boy for the mining boom, but why denigrate the thousands of workers who've committed to the disruption of a fly-in fly-out existence? Men and women slogging it out on twelve-hour shifts, knocking off for a half-life in a hot dusty town, a donga to call home, leaving families elsewhere to cope for long periods on their own.

How do newly affluent mine workers fit into our class structure? They'd give Karl Marx a nervous breakdown: wage slaves with nothing to lose but their gold chains? Revolutionaries with Rolexes? And let's not kid ourselves that class discrimination is dead – it's as common as a mock Prada handbag. There are always rich peoples' kids blushing at their Peppermint Grove addresses and ordinary people mocked for saying 'haitch'. (At parties in posh suburbs, that's 'haitch' as in 'hypocrisy.')

Guilt, anger, shame, pretence – few of us escape the confusions of class. And social climbers are everywhere (as they've always been) now driving leased Range Rovers and flashing their fake tans and fake personalities.

Perhaps my fantasy of a classless society is a fantasy in itself. I'd like to return to that time, not so long ago, when people were admired for what they did, not because they owned a weekender at Eagle Bay. That era before celebrity culture drove ego and reckless materialism into places it should never have gone – into schools and playgrounds. Last week I overheard a nine-year-old girl complaining to her mum: 'Jessica gets to go skiing in Japan, how come we only get to go to Bali?' A month ago, I asked my eldest what he wanted to be and he gave me a smirk and said 'rich'. He thought it was funny. I'm still not sure if he meant it.

I hope education, not affluence, opens the door to better lifestyles. We all want to choose our careers, not have the choice taken away by disadvantage. Snobbery amongst the younger set is usually nothing more than the parroting of their parents' pretension; of having no clue (and no curiosity) about how the other half lives. I hope my children learn early on that delusions of grandeur are more likely to make them an object of ridicule than an object of envy. And I want them to believe me when I tell them kindness and thoughtfulness will gain them respect far quicker than loading up on 'stuff' and showing off. Perhaps then, they'll end up in a class of their own.

MY PINING FOR PERFECTION

A haircut is not a trifling matter. This, men do not understand. To a man, a haircut is a way to kill fifteen minutes of a lunch hour. It involves no more mental taxation than reclining in a swivel chair arguing with a barber about Shane Warne's penchant for selfies.

For women, a haircut is the fastest route to an identity crisis. Period. It can coincide with that too. I should know – I just had one – a haircut, and a freak-out. Some people will no longer recognise me because I've gone short – I had a whole three centimetres cut off. For me, a change is nowhere near as good as a holiday.

Men should also know that women have a fraught relationship with their hair because hair is the only thing that can be changed at whim. And let's face it; most women grow up wanting to change everything about themselves. Well at least I did.

I was seven when I began noticing Serena down the road had a shiny blonde ponytail like Barbie, while I had limping stick-brown plaits like a Holly Hobby doll.

My downward comparisons got worse as I became a teenager. I measured myself against other girls according to blondeness or cascading wavy-ness – and was always left lacking and dissatisfied. It was the start of an uncomfortable relationship with being female, of wasting a significant portion of my young life sizing myself up against some narrow measure of the perfect woman's exterior.

I was in my twenties by the time I realised my insecurities were simply character weaknesses, and I could fix those. I decided that my negative body image was unhealthy and perverse, and I would no longer indulge it (except during 'that time of the month', when nothing is curable and there is no bright side).

Women have a peculiar knack for self-loathing, something I've rarely seen in a man. Really, it's a nauseatingly first-world problem — I'm sure if we had to rifle through a rubbish tip to find dinner or wash our clothes on a rock by the river, we wouldn't be giving two hoots about our hair. (We'd probably have sold it off to some merchant making fake hair extensions for the elaborately coiffed in Perth.)

Self-loathing is the flipside of self-obsession, two symptoms of that disease called vanity. Vanity must also be a side-effect of not having enough to do. I'm sure it's nice to always look flawless — but those who aspire to perfection must find themselves slave to an entirely joyless process. After all, a bad hair day can ambush even the most militant of beauty regimes.

I like to miss a few gym sessions and lose control at the smorgasbord because, well — because I can. My friends won't desert me and I like to imagine my husband will still think I'm a fox — he's seen me thin(ish) and also nine months pregnant, and hasn't passed judgment on either. (Smart men never do.)

The cult of female beauty is ingrained at an early age. In high school, I must have frittered away days of my life wishing for longer legs and less curves, obsessing over my Roman nose and muscly calves. I couldn't see anything but my faults. I was the sum total of a collection of ugly body parts.

Insecure as a teenager, I often mistook sexual harassment for compliments. Once, when the father of a girlfriend pinned me up against the wall of his shed after school, I felt flattered instead of repulsed. I look back on that day and still feel incredulous that my self-esteem was then propped on such flimsy scaffolding.

I had the best of role models – a mum who was confident, positive, and motivated to keep fit and eat well – no closet psychoses there. I had female teachers I admired and respected, aunties and friends' mothers I loved to bits who told me I was kind and intelligent, not pretty and thin. (I wished they'd said 'funny', because funny can compensate for all other shortfalls.)

I look back now and see I was much like every other girl, and every other girl was much like me: consumed with the glorified images of the impossibly glamorous models in our *Dolly* magazines. And yet as wives and mothers, when we're trying to stay sane juggling parenthood and working and caring for extended families, I find some women are still as competitive as ever. I don't get it – are they forever desperate to outshine the sisterhood? Is this relentless pursuit of perfection some misguided attempt at one-upmanship? What the blazes for? I can only surmise that there are women who need to feel envied to feel good about themselves. In my imperfect world, that looks to me like low self-esteem. Can't we all just admire each other?

I've decided the best test of a woman's vanity is a hideous haircut – the kind of haircut that you can see is a disaster even before they've finished drying it. I can recall the taste of rising panic as it dawned on me that the he-she with the scissors did his apprenticeship as a butcher, not as a hair 'artiste'. There I sat – (under that black plastic shroud that's always too tight around your neck) – struck mute by the dawning realisation that for the next three months, my new *do* would be the new *don't*. And when he'd finished his masterpiece, and I was looking as inviting as a soup sandwich, I got up and grinned stupidly: 'Thank you so much – no, no – really, I love it', handed over $150 and sobbed all the way home in the car. People who are vain are also smart enough to cause a scene belittling the hair-man so that at least they get a free disaster, and scare off all the other clients.

I have an impeccably stylish friend who claims hair, skin, weight and clothes, in that order, betray a woman's age. Oh dear, so boring hair now makes you look decrepit too? I've had it up to pussy's bow with stylers, straighteners and hot tongs. Those blasted appliances take up fifteen minutes of my sixteen-minute daily beauty regime. After all, it's just hair, it's not even alive, but it's the most demanding thing I own. And I expect it will be until I'm the owner of a perm and a blue rinse. At least then I'll take comfort in knowing the one upside to death will be never having to think about my hair.

THE WHISTLE STOP

Here is what I've learnt since taking up jogging: I do not run like a gazelle. Or a cheetah. Or any of those animals used as metaphors for people who can run fast and free. I run like Cliff Young. No-one will ever mistake me for an athlete.

Last week, as I pounded up the hill to the traffic lights, a young girl in hot-pink lycra ducked out of an apartment building and bounded onto the footpath ahead of me.

She looked as natural running as I do gossiping. I was mesmerised by her bottom. It was round and pert and muscular, and with each smooth stride her cheeks rose and fell like pistons. Her lean crankshaft-legs propelled her effortlessly forward. She was a machine. Nothing jiggled or rippled – this girl was poetry in motion, before it became a cliché.

As I jogged behind her, I saw part of the pavement had been blocked off by workmen restoring the council building on the corner. Two middle-aged blokes in fluoro vests were roping off one lane of the highway for pedestrians while half a dozen workmen screwed wooden scaffolding over the footpath.

I watched the damsel up ahead glide from the footpath to the cordoned-off lane and cruise past those workmen. Half a dozen hard hats on sunburnt necks swivelled in her direction. One fella elbowed a mate who was facing the wrong way. For several seconds, those construction workers were transfixed by the sight of my friend's air-cushioned bottom. As I got closer, I saw the foreman shaking his head in wonder. I chuckled as I thudded past him: 'Stop perving!'

'You're just jealous!' he shot back.

'You bet! But I'm ready for a wolf whistle!'

He snorted. 'You might be waiting a long time!'

A few seconds down the road, I glanced back at the building site to see who was ogling my 46-year-old rump. The foreman had turned his back to me and was telling a truck driver where to park. His workmates were clustered around a crane chaining beams to the hook. Up ahead the propeller-like ponytail of the girl-athlete was a blur. I could still make out the curves of her neon spandex that had caused such commotion among the blokes in blue singlets.

Sapped, I turned for home and slunk into the shower.

I wore hot-pink lycra once. I also wore white shorty-shorts with lace hems and a G-string leotard. This was my 6 am beach-walking outfit, because I was all class in the nineties. I'd power-walk from Scarborough to Floreat with a girlfriend in her purple leotard and micro-shorts. We were too busy gasbagging to notice anyone lusting after us. Or smirking.

But I do remember as a fourteen-year-old, there were two uni students who rented a cottage in the next street, a dozen houses up from my best friend. On summer Sunday afternoons, walking to her place to watch *Countdown*, I'd see those uni boys drinking beers, propped on their brick verandah. They'd call out: 'Come 'n have a beer with us! We won't bite!' Or they'd wolf whistle. Or wave.

They flummoxed me. Boys were scary. Were their bellows dangerous, like the mating calls of wildebeest? Were they just being neighbourly? Should I ignore them? Should I smile out of politeness, then walk faster? Or should I yell: 'Get nicked, losers!'

I smiled, then ignored them. It kept me virginal and in control. Our afternoon three-play became a contest. What would they yell out this time? 'Hey, babe, what's the rush? Where are you going? Can we come too?'

Years later, I bumped into one of them at a pub. Being less self-conscious, we laughed about those teasings. 'You were never rude to us' he said, 'We were just boofheads trying to get you to notice us. Hope you took it as a compliment'.

I told a girlfriend and she was furious: 'Men who wolf-whistle are judging women on their sexual attractiveness. You're not an object to be paraded for men's approval or disapproval!'

I've never heard workers on building sites voicing their *disapproval of women*. But yes, when I was young, I *was* intimidated. Sometimes I'd be frightened, and later, angry, if men's banter turned crude.

But then I confessed that I was crushed when those tattooed fellas at the building site showed no interest in my middle-aged bottom. My friend stared at me, horrified. And then I felt stupid and ashamed – like I'd sold out the sisterhood.

'I liked that foreman, the cheeky sod' I said. Those builders might have been smitten with that damsel's perfect derriere, but at least they showed their appreciation with silence.

I'm 46 now. I run like my knees are tied together. I have to stop after twenty-two minutes and my legs seize up in the car if I forget to stretch. So please Mr Foreman – give me some encouragement! Whistle at me! And make it loud. This would-be cougar needs something to brag about!

DON'T WORRY, I'LL GET AROUND TO IT, FOR SURE

Procrastination is the tiresome friend you wish you'd offloaded years ago. The kind of friend who needles you for being a hopeless ditherer.

Procrastination has been my snarky sidekick since I was a teenager. Back then, it was a slothful habit that turned exams into last-minute cramming sessions and assignments into all-nighters. Finally, high on adrenalin, I'd bash away on Mum's green Remington until 3 am, fingers stained a chalky grey from copious blots and smears of white-out.

Now I accept my ineptitude as a personality quirk. We tolerate each other, procrastination and I, in a spineless sort of way. We both know I still lack the mental grit to make my life more efficient.

I would have written about procrastination earlier, but it never seemed like the right time. Last week, during a sudden cloudburst, I sat down at my desk as the rain pelted down, determined to put procrastination in its place. I flipped open my laptop and up sprang a clean white screen. Through the window, a streak of sunlight skimmed the keyboard. I noticed a layer of dust collecting around the laptop's hinges.

An hour later, having dusted the whole house in a fit of pique, I sat back down. I typed five words on the page: *Procrastination is my worst enemy.* There! A start! But those words rubbed each other up the wrong way with their lumpy rhythm. I pressed delete and stared morosely as the screen emptied.

Looking up at the bamboo outside my window, I noticed a small cluster of ants gathering at the knot where a leaf branched out from the green stem. I searched the other branches for ant clumps. No, it was just this one hosting peak-hour ant traffic.

Every few seconds, an ant would separate from the clump and begin trekking down the plant, doing the usual meet-and-greet with another ant making her way up. (Worker ants are always *she,* Google tells me. Male ants are only good for sex – they laze about in the nest eating and making a mess and getting antsy waiting for their ant-sheilas to get home.)

I killed another half hour googling the study of myrme-cology. One scientist was claiming that the weight of all the humans on earth was the same as the weight of all the ants on earth. Ha! Not after I lose five kilos!

Given the chance, I can happily distract myself from serious tasks by trawling the internet. Google is a wormhole in the universe – time accelerates when you're faffing about looking up things you didn't know you were interested in. Suddenly, it's lunchtime. How did we waste time before computers?

The next morning, I wake up a day closer to deadline, feeling uneasy. I berate myself for wasting yesterday's free morning on dust and ants, and vow to knuckle down and finish the piece.

Then I spot the laundry bench spilling over with washing to be folded, and two loads of dirty socks and jocks waiting on the floor. A pile of bills is stacked by the phone. What to tackle first? Should I get the house in order or write about procrastination? Determined not to be waylaid again, I wedge my laptop under my arm, march out the front door and head for my local cafe. I tuck myself behind the back table, order a pot of tea and a chicken salad and wait for inspiration to find me.

Why do we allow ourselves to create pointless delays? Delays we know will make us worse off? Procrastination never made anyone happy: it's a vice, a completely irrational habit. We indulge in it against our better judgement. 'For goodness sake, get to work!' I tell myself.

While I fire up my laptop, I notice a young couple in furious discussion at another table. They're just out of hearing range but I'm fascinated by their body language. I can see she's on the defensive because she keeps shaking her head and her jaw is clenched. She has her arms folded and is leaning back in her chair. Her partner is pressing his bulk across the table to make his point: he's jabbing the air with his finger and spitting out his words. I start thinking about Nigella and Charles Saatchi and how mortified she must have been to have him grab her throat in public. Procrastination has me by the throat. Again.

Perhaps stress is the spark I need to ignite my brain. I can't just switch on my creative neurons at will. I have to be in the mood: preferably last-minute panic.

On the other hand, procrastination might be a necessary evil: it gives us the chance to incubate ideas, to mentally prepare for prize-winning brilliance. It might not be a time-wasting habit at all.

My salad arrives and the waitress points at my computer: 'Writer's block?' she asks with a grin.

'Yep' I sigh, 'but I'm planning to be spontaneously brilliant tomorrow'.

CHEWING THE FAT

A few weekends back a girlfriend and I were at the beach for our first swim of the summer. It was an overcast morning and the water looked dark. We were trying to stave off the inevitable shock of cold water by discussing our chances of getting eaten by a shark. She turned to me and said: 'Any self-respecting shark would take one look at me and say: Geez, I'm not *that* hungry.'

A real friend doesn't lie about her weight. A real friend understands that a woman's weight can be central to her mood: thin = happy, not thin = grumpy. My bathroom scales are an electronic slab of nastiness hell-bent on destroying my morning.

A nutritionist once told me: 'Do not weigh yourself every day, it's bad for your mental health.' But most mornings, I roll out of bed, skip to the loo and then step daintily onto my scales. It takes about three seconds for them to calculate how many squares of cooking chocolate I had the night before and deliver up the numbers that have me inwardly cursing (and outwardly cranky) for the next half hour.

If the figure is really offensive, I move the scales around the bathroom floor, hoping a second (or third) try will give me a more considerate read-out. Sometimes I hold onto the doorframe and voila! I weigh the same as I did when I was eighteen. Self-delusion makes me thin.

When I ring a girlfriend to say: 'Good morning, I am a circus tent', she doesn't reply: 'Hey, I've lost three kilos and I'm back to what I weighed on my wedding day.' Instead she sympathises: 'I weigh the same as the day I gave birth to my third child.'

My Adonis does not realise that all nearly all women obsess about their weight, usually to their partner's detriment. (The fatter we feel, the thinner our libido.)

Don't get me wrong; we're not so shallow that our weight is all we care about. We have discussed at length our disappointment that even the head of the CIA can't have an affair without getting caught. We worry Julia Gillard was talked into becoming a redhead by her hairdresser boyfriend. And then we go back to our weight, because society demands that the female of our species should always be pert and thin. Any woman who has had children or is within fifteen years of menopause knows pert requires surgery and pert *and* thin is a pipe dream.

I have two lovely pals who meet with me every Friday morning. Our husbands think it's a weekly discussion to exchange housekeeping tips, and how to serve up more marital happiness. But really, those girlfriends come to my house to find out what the scales of injustice say. Having starved ourselves all morning for 'weigh-in', the more sensible one of us records the offensive number of kilos in her diary. Then we put the bad news behind us and get down to the more important business of tea and cake.

I wouldn't miss those Fridays for quids. They began five years ago when we decided one of us might need a weekly catch-up to help her endure the horrors of chemotherapy. (We didn't need to weigh her to know she was thin.)

Since then there has been a wonderful survival story, one last baby, two husbands' vasectomies, two new places to live, one new career and several sets of hateful scales. Cancer free and in perfect nick, the most disciplined of our threesome now sympathises with the two of us whose blasted weight has stayed more or less the same, always five kilos too many.

We still debrief every Friday, except now we use 'weigh-in' as an excuse to check up on each other and restore some girly equilibrium.

What Friday weigh-ins are good for is motivation. The three of us come away hardened with steelier resolve to be Elle Macpherson-pure about what we eat. (Usually sabotaged by Troy Buswell-style self-control.) On occasion our iron will has lasted a whole week – the record is three months – but usually we're texting each other by Friday night: 'Do organic brownies count?' (Apparently, if they came from the health food shop, they have no calories.)

For me, trying to lose weight at this time of year is hopeless. And pointless. There are too many good things to eat. So I'm going to move those scales around the house until I find that elusive G-spot – G for gravity. That's the spot where a slight incline confuses the scale's pea-sized brain into thinking I'm three kilos lighter. I have high hopes for the bit of the kitchen floor that dips as it merges with the pantry. If my plan fails, I'll just use the stupid scales as a step-up to reach the top shelf. I'm sure that's where I hid the last of the cooking chocolate.

NEAR AND FAR

MEMORIES ARE HOUSED HERE

I am having a house-mourning.

With a sold sticker out the front, and the frenzy of home-opens behind us, we are moving on – our Federation cottage outgrown by a long-legged tween and a couple of smaller racket-makers. As settlement approaches, I have been reflecting on the meaning of nostalgia, and whether I suffer from it. You have to be a certain age to be nostalgic don't you? Nothing specific – just old enough to have lived enough to look back and feel sentimental. Or wistful. Or grateful.

I feel I ought to pay my respects to this house that has shepherded twelve years of my life and sheltered a new generation of my family – because I now know it as well as it knows me. How many times have I walked the jarrah boards of this hallway, the same boards that have echoed similar footsteps since 1907? I can tell you which boards still creak loud enough to scare the dead, though time and familiarity have softened the sudden heart thump I get when the floor cracks like a whip in the middle of the night. It's always my eldest padding to the loo.

I can share with you the history of a house built when cars were a novelty in Perth, when the city's population hit the magic mark of 30,000, and when tuckpointing and sash-windows were coveted by those who could afford bricks and mortar over weatherboard. I know these rooms later harboured a brothel – the West Leederville train stopped at the bottom of the street and those *in the know* would wander up past houses with dinner smells wafting in the air to score dessert with a one-night wife. (A hundred years later, this house is so disorderly most days it could still pass as a brothel.)

I can talk you through the life cycle of the elm tree in the backyard, having watched this very week the first two leaves spring to life off a skeleton of bare branches. The tree the kids went wild over last Christmas when Uncle Andy strung it with fairy lights. The summer canopy that cools off the back deck by 3 pm but drives us nuts in autumn when it blankets the lawn with fallen leaves – we draw straws to see who lands the seemingly endless task of raking them up.

I can also bring to mind that afternoon two years ago when a massive storm sent a lightning bolt down the trunk of the gum tree out front, shorting the whole street and exploding branches all over the verge. I thanked the house that night when the rain fell so hard I was sure the gutters would give up, but didn't. The night we couldn't hear ourselves speak from the deafening torrent on the tin roof. The one we still laugh about as the only night our new baby daughter slept through.

My house has carried me through the tumultuous years of pregnancy and small babies, first steps and first days at school. I have finger-smeared photos on the fridge of little boys in new uniforms sitting expectantly on the verandah steps. I can remember their excitement at having scrawled their initials in the soft cement out the front as the council laid a new footpath. (The workmen kindly turned a blind eye.) Or living through the chaos of month after month of renovations, then panicking when the painters were all set and I still couldn't decide which tester pot I liked best.

As far as I can tell, nostalgia does not like remorse for company, or shame, or bitterness – the unfortunate but sometimes unavoidable downtimes of a human existence – low points strung randomly between the day-to-day loops of life. Those things are best tucked away and revisited as little as possible. Regret is not for sentimental retrieval.

Why do we feel nostalgic? What is the evolutionary point of the recollection of powerful emotions? Is it so we can regret those feelings that are no longer with us? So we can mark the passage of 'time lived'? What about painful memory? Can we still call it nostalgia if we reminisce about the traumas of past illness, the pain of lost love?

I hope I will retain the mental agility to look back on eighty, if I'm lucky ninety, years on this planet as well lived. Will I still be able to recall, and, more importantly, draw pleasure from, the faint memories of childhood, blurry chapters of another life, a smaller one – the new-car smell of the red upholstery in my grandmother's Morris 1100? Or remember the feel of her as I gave her a tight hug and felt stiff bones – not hers but the Playtex girdle's.

Strangely, I cannot recall her voice, or her laugh. She must have taken them with her. But I know smell is a potent reviver of memory. I can recall in a flash the perfume of her bright pink lipstick in its gold case, or the powdery scent of her makeup. Can we really memorise smells? In 2009, scientists discovered that childhood smells have a 'privileged' position in our memories, that they bypass the usual sensory processing stations in the brain to be stored deep as primary impulses. That might explain why memories triggered by smells are more vivid and emotional than those triggered by words, sounds or pictures.

What will my children remember of this house? What deep-seated impressions will it leave on their memories? I hope it's the smell of their birthday cakes in the oven, or the scent of the jasmine in flower as they brush past it on the narrow path around the back. Or the sun-baked joy of the first summer we spent in our new pool, bypassing the beach for an inflatable shark.

Home is primal: somewhere we feel safe, and familiar, and in control. No wonder moving house is a stressful life event – I already feel uncomfortable, bereft even, knowing I am about to lose my sense of 'belonging' – a decade of knowing most people in our street by name, my children's favourite playmates across the road, our houses interchangeable on any given day, each almost as familiar as their own.

I wonder when we're old, if we tell our life stories realistically or nostalgically, if we embellish them to make them more interesting, or censor our misdemeanours to save our pride? My mother's stories from her childhood have the glow of halcyon days – I know the stories I tell my children of high school have the rough edges smoothed over. How do we present our history to others? How will I set the bones of this house for re-telling to others?

My youngest won't remember her first home – it'll be up to her dad and me, and her big brothers, to regale her with all the funny stories we collected here. Instead, the memories of her childhood will be laid down, year by year, in another century-old home in another suburb not far from here, a house (with stairs!) preparing itself for the onslaught of our family.

And what of this old Federation dame left behind, who has looked after us so well? I'm delighted to tell you we've sold to a couple with a toddler and a baby on the way, a young family whom I hope will revel in a new chapter in the history of number 38 – a new cycle of 'belonging'. May they create for themselves a houseful of lovely memories just as we have. To be packed up and taken with us for the sake of nostalgia.

MORE THE MERRIER IN FAMILY TERRITORY

Sometimes, a two-hour drive is all it takes to turn humdrum to holiday.

'How about a romantic weekend away?' my Lothario whispers across his pillow, our love life handicapped by the three-year-old octopus suckered between us.

'Just a couple of days hey?' he murmurs. 'Somewhere exotic. By the beach. Away from all this.'

I could have kissed him. Instead, my arm is paralysed by the dead weight of a sleeping child's leg-tentacle flopped across my chest.

'Promise?' I whisper back.

'No', comes the reply, 'but the weekend after next I have to go to my high-school reunion in Bunbury. I've booked us all into the Lord Forrest hotel.'

Those who remember Alan Bond will recall his gift to Bunbury: a five-storey shiny white high-rise with a single porthole window skewered through its pointy apex. Driving into town last weekend, Bondy's tower loomed over the back beach like the snout of a white pointer. Its dark porthole eye followed me all the way to the hotel carpark.

'It doesn't look like a shark, dopey!' says my husband. 'It's supposed to look like the prow of a ship!'

'Well I say it's a shark!' (much like its owner in 1983).

So here I am at the Lord Forrest, sitting on a plastic patio chair by the side of the once-famous atrium pool, staring up at the hanging gardens of Bunbury (devil's ivy).

'Mum!' cries my six-year-old. 'There's a bridge! And pretend rocks! And a waterfall! And look! You can see through the roof!'

Outside the rain is sheeting down, but my children are intoxicated by their first taste of three-and-a-half star luxury. Small son plays hopscotch on the crazy paving, mindful not to step on the cracks. Then he discovers a blue button in the wall and leaps in fright when the spa gurgles to life. His sister flaps her inflatable orange arms and paddles over to the pretend-rock steps for a closer look.

The pool gate swings open and in walks a portly bloke in baggy shorts, flanked by two primary-school-aged granddaughters.

The girls leap into the water and the granddad settles himself at the only poolside table – mine.

'Nice day for swimming!' he says and we laugh politely.

I can see through the lobby windows a row of date palms flailing in the squall outside.

'Frank!' he says, by way of introduction, and pumps my hand. 'Travelled far?'

'Just from Perth. It's my husband's thirty-year school reunion tonight. He's up in the room deciding which side to part his hair.'

'Ha!' he snorts. 'We're holidaying close to home this time. My wife has a sore hip. We're doing the wineries, sixteen of us.'

'Sixteen?' I say, thinking he must be on a tour.

'Yeah, the whole family. We do all our holidays together – two daughters, their husbands, my son, his wife, the grandkids – eleven of them.'

I must look incredulous because he adds: 'Yep, we're the Griswold clan. We travel in convoy. We need five cars – the eldest grandkid is nineteen and they tail down to three.'

'Wow!' is all I can manage.

'Yeah, we've seen the world all right. Last year we went on a cruise through the Caribbean, we did Greece and Turkey before that. We've gone from one side of America to the other. Sometimes we take up four rows on the plane.'

'Why?' (I feel a hermit by comparison.) 'Doesn't everyone want to do their own thing?'

'Sometimes. But this way, the kids learn how to be part of a tribe. We learn about them. I can tell you, that one there…' – he points to the elder girl in the pool – 'she's only nine but she'll do anything for anyone. Her cousin, she's six – smart as a whip. Best speller in her class.'

I see the pride on his face. He shrugs at me and grins, as if all families are like his.

I try to picture my family, en masse, checking in at Air Bulgaria. All those niggling, squawking personalities trying to control proceedings: dominators, peace-makers, martyrs. Didacts, autocrats, me – dreaming of an upgrade.

'Is it relaxing?' I ask.

'Most of the time. Neutral territory helps. We use these holidays to catch up on everyone. I want to know what the young ones are thinking, how they see the world. In return, we tell the grandkids all the old family stories – remind them how they got here.'

I wonder if I tell my children enough about their past. Do they understand the world had its own momentum before they arrived? That they belong to something bigger than themselves?

Frank's granddaughters have climbed out of the pool and are shivering. He stands up and hands them each a towel.

'What'll we do now, Granddad?'

'Let's go and see what the others are up to!' He winks at me, then raises his hand in a gentlemanly salute: 'You can never separate who you are from where you're from.'

And with that, the pool gate clangs shut behind them.

SAVED BY THE SISTERHOOD

The sisterhood is one of my most precious possessions. After children and the love of a husband. (Though sometimes my girlfriends understand me in ways he couldn't imagine.)

It's not just about the X-chromosome. My metaphorical sisters have been my lifelong companions, a good handful of them since I was fifteen. They have been in and around my life, often daily, for thirty years or more and rarely have we had a cross word. We have been through awful boys and lovely ones, broken hearts and narrow escapes, white weddings, the blackness of divorce, grand achievements and career stalls, the trauma of death, exhilarating births and the terrible trials of the tracksuit years – those seemingly endless days when babies and small children left you with no fashion sense save for the trackie daks you thought hid all the sins of procreation, but didn't.

The sisterhood has been created for all women to dip into whenever and wherever they need it. Some are quite self sufficient and only need a couple of its members on occasion, others like a whole tribe, in constant communication. Some you keep at arm's length, and some are your bosom buddies for life. You can never be too giving. But you can be too demanding. Sometimes, the truest marker of a friendship is seeing how much it can withstand.

I have one who reads this column before you do, just to make sure I'm not making a fool of myself. That could test a friendship, but she dishes out constructive criticism like expensive perfume – it packs a punch but then drifts to a soft finish. Our friendship has reached new levels of trust.

Do men have this intensity of friendship? I hope my husband does, though the evidence is sparse, and couched in rhyming slang and blokey deadpans. I'm not clear if it gets much deeper than that. Who knows how many men discuss the things (we hope) are most important to them – the state of their relationships, worries about children, careers, whether their wives are pulling their weight around the house. On nights out I ask him: 'What did you talk about?' and he'll reply: 'football, Ricky Ponting throwing in the towel, man-opause', and I'll reply: 'How's such-and-such's wife? And children?' And he'll say: 'Dunno. Didn't ask.'

Male friendships are the unthinkable female ones – the kind that if you didn't ask about someone's husband or children, or how their job was going, you'd never be invited out to a girls' lunch again. Perhaps men just don't want to waste time weaving over and under the same emotionally fraught subject until someone finally breaks the deadlock and says: 'Okay, it's settled. Wear the red one.'

Is the much-celebrated tradition of Australian mateship, with its ribald humour and jocular put-downs, as alive and well and living in the suburbs as it was for the diggers, and drovers, the shearers and bushrangers? When men yarned over a pint in the pub, or spent a larrikin's Saturday helping a mate move house, or worse, building one. I think mateship is as shipshape as ever, it's just that the business and busy-ness of men's lives got in the way.

I think for that reason, men's friendships are about escapism. Of being freed from work and responsibilities to have a belly laugh with mates who keep their angst to themselves and enjoy the process of looking outwards onto the world. I think I envy them. They don't obsess like we do. Women often churn inwards, needing to share experiences in mindblowing detail in the safety of the cone of silence. There really are few secrets left amongst us. Men are much more careful about thinking out loud.

My most cherished witch's coven (as the man of the house lovingly refers to us) likes to get together every so often, the three of us, for what we call 'committee meetings'. At these, we discuss the order of the day, usually a crisis for one of us that requires three heads, wine and speaking in tongues. By hour's end, and divination, we have usually solved most of the world's curses (like teenagers, and G-strings) and why husband A prefers not to have deep-and-meaningfuls about his marriage at three in the morning? Why not, we argue? It's quiet, the kids are asleep. And what does he mean, 'She's a succubus?'. (I had to look it up, too).

Those girls, and the lovely others I have collected over the years, have been my saviours so many times, they are the sisters I never had. I don't know if life would be as rich and varied without them. Certainly, I have laughed with them so hard and so often that they are like endorphins. I crave their company.

A true female friendship can withstand as many ongoing conversations as there are participants. You can be in earnest discussion with one, whilst keeping an ear on another and be able to make insightful interjections into a third. We are talented in so many ways. A man has a conversation in as few words as possible. And you're a best mate if you can keep quiet and nod in sympathetic silence.

Women need their friends because men don't appreciate the sheer effort required to keep a conversation going at warp speed. Brain and mouth at full pelt, no filter required. I have left girls' lunches satiated but exhausted from the mental gymnastics of trying to get through everyone's news in under a lunch hour. I hope that men appreciate the sisterhood for taking the pressure off their ears.

My mother has a precious collection of her own, a circle of girl(ish) seventy-somethings, who through thick and thin have stuck by each other for near on six decades, and are as close as ever. Rarely grumpy, always empathetic, generous of spirit, they have looked after each other in sickness and in health, and the vows of friendship have stuck fast through the terrible times and more often than not, the joys of a well-lived life. My mum has reminded me more than once that my girlfriends will be there for me even when the men in my life aren't. And so right she has been.

The sisterhood inspires because it is as varied as its members are clever, and funny, and breathtakingly gorgeous, inside, where it counts. And I feel about them the way I feel when separated from my children. Like I'm missing a body part. Legless. They're good for that too.

HELLO STRANGER, I'VE JOINED THE 'HOOD

Moving neighbourhoods is a test of my social skills. I knew the shift would be a wrench: How could we replace our favourite family across the road? Three brothers under nine who shimmy like monkeys up their wrought-iron fence and hang on the crossbars yelling: 'Hello! Hello! Can you come and play?'

Our three would send back an equally ear-splitting chorus of greetings (while taking turns to ride the gate off its hinges). We two mothers would leave surprises at each other's doors – a bunch of parsley, or my latest attempt at low-fat brownies. (Why bother, we decided). On chaotic mornings, I could signal a mayday from the porch and she would walk my boys to school.

Two doors up, the mum of another trio of boys would share with me her recipe for lemon cupcakes and raising twelve-year-olds. Her bags of hand-me downs outfitted my eldest son for years.

Further along was the Italian nonna who gushed over my babies and leant on her rake explaining to me the old ways of bottling homemade tomato sauce and how to stop basil going to seed. On weekends, the kids would flash past her on their bikes bellowing: 'Ciao Ciao Pina!' Or they'd call up to her as she dusted the Doric columns of her Juliet balcony: 'Can we practice our scooter tricks on your driveway?' (She has a spotless expanse of concrete.)

I don't like putting barriers around my family. They should feel safe by instinct. I want my children to have the same freedoms I had growing up in the 1970s, when we knew almost everyone in the street by name and the neighbourhood kids roamed as a motley tribe. I don't want my children being fearful of strangers. I like it when people stop at our fence to ask my five-year-old: 'Was that your big boy's bed arriving this morning? How'd they get it through your door?'

We have been in our new house for four months now, and our old suburb is becoming a faded postcard. Now I need to memorise another footpath for potholes and jutting pavers that could tip up a scooter or skin the knees of a budding skateboarder.

Diagonally opposite our century-old cottage, there's another wrought-iron fence and three little faces curious to see who has moved in. I feel the throb of awkwardness and insecurity as I make the first tentative offers of friendship. But the kids hit it off and we are away! Within a fortnight small children are madly swapping houses – and we two mums discover we have a girlfriend in common.

I'm heartened by the elderly couple who cross the road to say to me: 'You'll love it here.' The neighbours on the west side say: 'It's so good to hear children in the backyard again.'

Uprooting forces me to be resilient. The kids dream up the idea of walks after tea in their pyjamas. I make a point of smiling and talking to everyone we meet. I would never have had such confidence before motherhood. But a gregarious small daughter and two excitable boys make conversation-starters easy: 'Why are you wearing that funny hat?' asks my small daughter of an elderly lady sweeping her path. The lovely old dear replies: 'You know what? It hides my funny hair.'

Near and Far

After a weekend of work at the family farm, we bring home a load of fallen apples and juicy Meyer lemons. The kids want to make the 'deliveries' they enjoyed in the previous suburb. They laboriously count out a dozen Fujis, still with leaves attached, and add a couple of lemons to each bag. Five-year-old son proudly draws a tree dotted with red splodges and writes: 'Wood you lik some fresh appels from our farm? XX from us.'

We leave our surprise bags at front doors without being spotted. Within the week we have several handwritten thank-yous in the letter box. The kids are delighted.

There are shopkeepers to befriend too. We five become Dave the Icecream Man's best customers. While the small ones deliberate over cups or cones, Dave and I discover we once lived in the same street.

I feel at home. The kids are settled, the neighbourhood is becoming familiar – apart from one decrepit old fella who makes two round trips past our house each day. Is he shuffling to the shops? He always returns empty-handed. No hello, just a grunt. And then one lunchtime, he takes a tumble at our gate. Blood is dripping from his papery hand. We bundle him home to number 39 in the car. Without a word, he lurches inside, leaving his startled wife to make apologies.

The next morning he stops at our gate as I'm unloading the car. He extends a bandaged right hand: 'I'm Milton', he says gruffly. 'Had one too many at the bowling club yesterday.'

The kids now yell out 'Hi Milton!' If he hears them, he raises his hand but his eyes remain firmly on the pavement. Neighbourhoods embrace all types.

FAST TRAIN TRACK TO NOWHERE

Train travel is the ultimate vehicle for people watching. It's the perfect antidote to the four-walled claustrophobia of housewifery. I like to feel part of the throng to-ing and fro-ing, strangers heading briefly in the same direction.

On my way to the station, I cast my eye over the dozen commuters up ahead on the platform. Everyone does their waiting in their own way. No-one looks agitated or out of breath, so I conclude we haven't just missed the train.

My three-year-old daughter scrambles out of her stroller to empty her ten-cent coin collection into the ticket machine. A dishevelled young bloke with wild hair and no shoes shuffles past us. He settles himself down in a patch of sunlight strobed by the wooden bench and closes his eyes. For a moment, my toddler stops feeding the machine while she studies his face.

'Hit the jackpot yet?' An elderly gent in a tweed jacket has strolled up behind us. As the last of the ten-cent pieces clunk down the slot, small daughter fishes for the ticket as it drops into the tray. 'I winned!' she yells, waving her prize in the air.

We crane our necks to see who'll be first to spot our train snaking round the bend. We hear the hiss of metal brakes and soon after four carriages rumble into the station.

I always turn left once inside the doors, just to imagine the thrill of first class travel. Three-year-old, kneeling on her seat, presses her face against the window. I settle in for the ride to town, trying to guess where my travelling companions are going and why.

Next to me is a nerdy-looking bloke wearing Woody Allen glasses. He holds his smartphone in his lap and texts: 'Be there soon, darling.' I feel guilty reading over his shoulder, but I can't help myself. I wonder if he's texting a lover, a girlfriend or his wife. I settle on 'girlfriend' and picture her as Annie Hall in wide-legged woollen pants and fedora hat.

Opposite us are two middle-aged women talking in sign language. I am mesmerised. In between bouts of furious hand movements they throw back their heads and laugh raucously. Their merriment is the only human sound in our carriage.

Everyone else has their head bowed, fixated by the gadgets in their laps. There's not a book or newspaper in sight. No-one is talking, or taking in the view. There is only quiet concentration as thumbs sweep over keypads. Technology is hard at work here.

I'm struck by the notion of eye contact, and what has happened to it. There's certainly none in this carriage. Even the three teenagers huddled by the door are isolates bent over their devices. They are strangely expressionless, oblivious to their surroundings. A businessman standing near them stumbles and grabs for the handhold as the train brakes start to grip – but not one of the teenagers look up. Twice he has to say 'excuse me' before they begrudgingly move aside to let him off.

Perhaps the virtual world makes reality dull by comparison. But I remember the bus ride home from high school as the highlight of my school days. The novelty of having boys on board sent our girly chatter into hyper-drive. One sly smile from a cute boy would provide endless entertainment. We would duck behind our seats giggling, then dissect his body language so intently we thought we could read his mind before he even spoke it. ('Can you reach the bell for me?' became as exciting as a first kiss.)

Yesterday, at my favourite corner cafe, I was puzzled by two young women having coffee at a nearby table. They looked to me like old pals, but for several minutes, they sat in silence, absentmindedly punching their thoughts into their phones. Perhaps connecting on Facebook is more fun than connecting across the table, I thought. But it was an odd sight. What's driving this obsession? Fear of missing out? On what? The rapid-fire rush of social networking.

At dinner I tell my eldest son about my train ride. I recount for him what it was like before smartphones and iPods. How I would catch buses and trains and have no choice but to kill time watching the passing parade of commuters or the slideshow of suburbs flitting by. I tell him I quite enjoyed the downtime after the frenetic pace of the newsroom.

I wonder out loud whether we're all more productive for having the internet as our constant and available companion. Whether this ever-present connectedness is making us super-efficient. And are we happier for it? My son pipes up: 'Maybe those people on the train were just plain bored, Mum.'

That got me thinking. Dead time is now considered a waste of time. Portable technology fills the quiet gaps in living and keeps us permanently switched on and plugged in. Perhaps that's why I love forgoing the car for the train: someone else to do the driving. Twenty minutes of mental holiday. That's what I crave.

OH DANNY BOY, YOU'RE HOMESICK

A homesick Irishman is the last person you expect to find on a storm-wrecked Swanbourne beach on a Sunday morning. It was not yet 8 am and the wind was biting. As the kids and I climbed over the craggy rocks jutting out over the point, we spotted a middle-aged dad and his two small boys down in the cove. They were fossicking about in the great mounds of seaweed coughed up by the still-surging ocean.

My three kids were keen to see what mysterious flotsam those boys were collecting in their buckets. So the dad and I got talking. His wife was sleeping off a nurse's nightshift, he told me, and his boys needed to blow off steam. My own husband had just flown in from the Philippines, I told him, and we'd abandoned the house so he could enjoy his jetlag in peace.

'Ryan!' he introduced himself, and crushed my hand in his. We laughed at the lunacy of a trip to the beach on a day like this. He'd come prepared to be weather-beaten: his boys were in woolly turtlenecks zipped inside windcheaters. They were sloshing about in knee-high welly boots, beanies pulled down low to cover small ears.

My boys had refused to wear anything but board shorts. Three-year-old daughter had agreed to a tracksuit, but was saturated within a few minutes. She stripped down to her knickers and a singlet and began collecting shells, flashing her goosebumps at the weak-willed sun.

I had to concentrate to decipher Ryan's south Dublin brogue as the wind snatched his words and flung them past my ears: 'Y'knaw, there was nothin' doin' at home', he said. 'We'd been to Australia on holiday and I loved the place, milk n' honey, like. We came out eighteen months ago. It was my idea to move – I landed a job in construction.'

'How have you found it here?' I asked.

'Ay, I like it, but not enough. I think we have to go home soon', he said, scuffing the sand with his left boot, 'My wife is desperately homesick – she's not managing well.'

'What are you missing most?'

'Green fields, family, the neighbours.'

'In that order?' I laughed, and he nodded.

'My wife has twenty-seven nieces and nephews all about, and the neighbours, we're very close with the neighbours. The village comes alive after knock-off – we head in next door or up the lane for a couple of pints while the kids play. You don't do that here – I miss it.'

That got me thinking. Is homesickness a weakness? I always thought homebodies who stay rooted to the same familiar place must lack ambition or curiosity. But then I experienced the wrench of dislocation for myself.

At age twenty-six, I was distraught with homesickness after moving to Sydney for a new job. It was meant to be summer, but the rain bucketed down. My excitement soon wore off and I slid into despondency.

Home was a rented flat in an unfamiliar suburb. Work colleagues were indifferent to the new girl. On weekends, I became a lonely observer of other people's happiness. I traipsed around my new city on foot. In sidewalk cafes, I was the solitary figure contemplating the parade of couples and families. It seemed everyone but me took the comforts of belonging for granted. I never quite shook that feeling of restlessness. The dull ache of homesickness stayed with me even as I made a new life in a city I grew fond of. Four years later, I seized the opportunity to move back to Perth.

Now I question whether my homesickness was a deficiency: me, pining for home, because I couldn't cope with the newness of being alone.

Fifteen years later, I fantasise about escaping the stranglehold of my domestic responsibilities and moving the five of us to some exotic locale. I fool myself into believing I could be at home anywhere in the world. After all, I could instantly reconnect with friends on Skype and Facebook, family would be just a text or a mouse-click away. Such are my daydreams. Technology may have created the global village but it cannot convince me migration is now painless.

I ask my perpetually jetlagged husband if he struggles with homesickness when he's away. 'Always', comes the reply.

'What does it feel like?'

'Melancholy', he says, 'Waves of it. And talking on the phone just reminds me of what I'm missing'.

Homesickness must be a close relative of nostalgia. We are not easily separated from the people and places who shape our histories. The Irishman on the beach could not explain his wife's deep longing for the green fields of Delgany. But even I knew a balding Australian paddock was a poor substitute.

'My wife comes from a family of twelve', he tells me. 'It's not easy leaving that behind.'

'Twelve?' I gasp. 'My husband's one of seven and I thought that was a big family! He and his younger brother are born in the same year!'

'Aah', he replies, 'back home we call them Irish twins'.

GIVING UP THE WORST WEAKNESS

Failure is not my friend, but I've got used to its company over the years. It has been shadowing me at a quiet distance since I was a kid, biding its time until I tripped up or blundered, then gleefully trumpeting my wrong turns and dead-end decisions. Failure has made a fool of me on plenty of occasions and brought me to my knees on others.

Most people like to measure themselves by their successes, but it's their failings that are far more illuminating. I like to look back on mine as faint imprints on the stepping stones I've used to go places. They signal turning points in my life – those humiliating times when I made an ass of myself, or was blindsided by hubris. Minor defeats were annoying reminders of why I needed to try harder, or get smarter. In truth, my career began with a succession of failures.

It took me years to get into journalism in the 1980s, long before there was a university degree of the same name to carry under my arm to job interviews. Back then knocking on doors was an acceptable entry route, but few bosses saw any potential in me. I was too naive, too unsure of myself. I don't really know what I *wasn't*; I was just wet behind the ears, I suppose. I never thought to trade favours on my father's newspaper pedigree – that would have involved the shame of having to explain why I didn't know my absent dad, so a career in print was not an option.

Instead, I got part-time jobs writing the funnies for breakfast radio and being the ditzy barrel girl (scatterbrained required no acting at twenty) until finally, the news editor got fed up being harassed on the way to the loo and let me join the newsroom. I loved the business of writing hourly bulletins on the run, dashing from the printer to the tiny sound-proofed booth to read the news, chasing tip-offs and ambulances, but it was telling stories with moving pictures that I really hankered after.

Trying to make the transition from radio to television meant getting rejected in newer and more painful ways. I spent a year working for peanuts, making cups of tea, doing the photocopying. News directors would sigh and give me another weary: 'Nah, nothin' going.' Or better still: 'Come back when someone else has given you a crack.' Every knockback throbbed for a few days until I resolved to test my bruised ego again, each time that little bit more desperate to get noticed. When the ABC finally took a punt on me, I was twenty-three, and tenacity had become my middle name.

TV is a fickle business – if you're in front of the camera you live and die at the whim of executives who decide if you're watchable (whatever that means). Management bigwigs change as often as rating seasons and those new to the job of hiring and firing like to make their mark by axing programs, boning has-beens or elevating no-ones into some-ones. It's a cruel business for wannabes and also-rans, but a favourite Chief of Staff once told me: 'You haven't made it in television until you've been sacked at least once.'

Once was all it took – age thirty-one – I was fired from my hosting job three weeks after having my first baby. No-one ever said why, but getting shafted on maternity leave meant hiring lawyers and going into battle, if only to preserve what shreds remained of my dignity. There was an out-of-court cash settlement, but psychologically, I was devastated (post-natal and devastated). It was a terrible start to motherhood.

That sacking taught me how ruthless and disloyal people could be, and the identity crisis that followed floored me with self-doubt. I found out who my real friends were, and who was dining out on my misfortune. But I also learnt why the greatest weakness is in giving up. I sat at home for six months adoring my new baby and acknowledging my shortcomings. Rock bottom isn't a bad place to be when you realise there's nowhere lower to go. The thing I feared most had happened to me, but I had survived my fall from grace and discovered strengths I didn't know I had. So I dusted myself off and spent the next twelve years on other programs, taking on tougher roles than I ever imagined myself capable of.

I know my children need to taste failure sooner or later, the eldest one especially. But that's a politically incorrect thing to say when many parents today prefer to clear the obstacles in their children's path. I see it in my own parenting sometimes, that tendency to want to spare my children the pain of failure. And I remind myself to step back and let them fall.

Maybe it's persistence I need to teach my children. I see them wanting to give up at the first sign of struggle, or trying to bow out as soon as they realise they're not a natural at something new. I wonder if failure is often about arrogance too, because the smart set likes to imagine that hard work and doggedness are for upstarts who aren't gifted by birth. Show ponies expect to wake up one day and be an overnight success. (Actually, they've got it half right, because invariably, they will wake up.)

I checked with my bloke about his failures: 'Haven't had any.'

'Don't be silly, what about failed relationships?'

'Haven't had any.' (Perhaps self-delusion can be as rewarding as conceit.)

Stupidly, I pressed him further: 'Well, what have *my* failures been?' That got him going: 'Failure to get the message, failure to do what you're told.'

Society now considers failure as some sort of deficiency. 'Failure is not an option' is the new mantra for mavericks and up-and-comings. I subscribe to J. K. Rowling's thoughts on defeat, as she reflected on a time when her marriage was over and her wizard Harry Potter had been rejected by a dozen publishers: 'It's impossible to live without failing at something, unless you live so cautiously that you might as well not have lived at all – in which case, you fail by default.'

I don't know many people who readily accept that the breakdown of their marriage was a failure of their own making – it's usually the wicked spouse who's blamed. That's the escape clause we use so often to excuse our failures: watering down the facts and re-telling our histories gets us off the hook – and offloads the burden of responsibility.

Agreeing to write this column was my biggest risk in several years: not least because it'd be my first foray into newspapers. The editor told me: 'Your brief is to write of an ordinary life at home.' I set out to write a column from a woman's perspective that a man would want to read. I worried that you would think less of me the more I wrote, that your dismissal would be like a rejection of my take on life: an awful prospect. But whether you desert me next week, or stick by me with your lovely emails and encouragement, I will keep trying to be fearless and honest. I may later regret some of the things I've written, but at least the regretter will be an older and wiser version of myself. I'm a veteran of failure, but I'll take a risk on your tolerance.

ACKNOWLEDGEMENTS

Thank you to my old friend and editor Colleen Egan, for the gift of opportunity and for your unwavering support.

To Terri-ann White, for embracing this book and for your wisdom, patience and gracious ways.

I am grateful to my Weekend West Magazine editors, Julie Hosking and Amanda Keenan, for your keen eyes, your tolerance and for letting me roam free.

To Jan Martin, John Cunningham, Jane Simpson and Melanie Naylor: for your rigorous reading (and re-reading), your encouragement, your sometimes painful honesty and for your loyal friendship.

This book would not have been possible without the mentorship of my father, Tony Thomas, who has given unstintingly of his time, his writerly expertise and his perfectionist gene.

And to my dearest Mum, my bedrock – thank you for your infectious optimism, your tireless encouragement and for backing me at every turn.

Lastly, I don't know how to thank my husband, Matt – to whose opinion I am addicted.

www.ingramcontent.com/pod-product-compliance
Lightning Source LLC
Chambersburg PA
CBHW032034150426
43194CB00006B/266